D1267504

Exchange Traded Funds

A Concise Guide to ETFs

By Francis Groves

Hh

HARRIMAN HOUSE LTD

3A Penns Road
Petersfield
Hampshire
GU32 2EW
GREAT BRITAIN

Tel: +44 (0)1730 233870
Fax: +44 (0)1730 233880
Email: enquiries@harriman-house.com
Website: www.harriman-house.com

First published in Great Britain in 2011

Copyright © Harriman House Ltd

The right of Francis Groves to be identified as the author has been asserted in accordance with the Copyright, Designs and Patents Act 1988.

978-1-906659-14-1

British Library Cataloguing in Publication Data
A CIP catalogue record for this book can be obtained from the British Library.

Printed and bound in Great Britain by CPI Antony Rowe, Chippenham and Eastbourne.

Contents

About the author

Francis Groves studied modern history at the London School of Economics and has many years of experience working for legal and financial publishers including Reuters, the *Financial Times* and Butterworths. He has written on overseas property investment and created financial literacy training materials. The interaction of politics and finance is a particular interest for him. Francis enjoys reading history and walking in his spare time.

Preface

What the book covers

This is an introduction to exchange traded funds (ETFs), the latest generation of collective investments. The aim of this book is to show how ETFs are constructed, the way they work and the different asset classes ETFs now cover.

The main focus of the book is on ETFs that track indices, as these are undoubtedly the most important in terms of their range, the amounts of money invested and the advantages they offer. Further, every ETF's performance is inextricably linked to the index it tracks. The principle that to understand an ETF it is also necessary to thoroughly understand the underlying index is a key theme of this guide and the workings of several kinds of index are examined.

The range of ETFs described here include those tracking indices for equities, fixed interest securities, money markets, currencies, credit markets, property and commodity futures. ETFs offering methods of imitating hedging strategies are also explained, together with the new generation of **active** (as opposed to index tracking) **ETFs**. Of these ETFs for various asset types, by far the most important are those that track equities. For this reason, the main focus of this book is on equities and readers should assume that the book is referring to equity ETFs unless otherwise stated. For more on the prevalence of equity ETFs see 'A perspective on the different ETF asset classes' on page xiii.

Most of the ETFs covered in this book are listed on the London Stock Exchange (LSE). However, most ETF providers are not UK businesses and most London-listed ETFs are domiciled in other European Union (EU) member states (which means the ETFs are legally registered outside the UK). For this reason, careful attention has been paid to the European Union and UK regulatory framework that ETFs operate under. At points throughout the book I refer to *European ETFs* – these ETFs are available to UK investors, but since they are regulated in the same way throughout the EU it is helpful to refer to them as European ETFs (as distinct from American ETFs, which are regulated differently). This distinction between European and American ETFs is important because one of the broadest divisions between types of ETFs is that between those in Europe and America – the history of ETFs, their regulation and how the funds operate is different in the US.

This does not mean we will ignore American ETFs altogether. Two of the most important ETF providers in the UK are American companies – Blackrock iShares and Invesco Powershares. Also, many of the important developments in ETFs have taken place in the United States and many of the cutting edge ETF refinements are taking place there. This being the case, the guide provides the American context to important ETF developments.

Who the book is for

The book is for professional investors, financial advisors and others involved in the finance industry who need a basic overview of the ETF world.

ETFs are explained in a way that will make sense to those who are conversant with portfolios of individual stocks or retail products such as investment funds, but this guide will be equally accessible to those whose investments are entirely made up of exchange traded products.

How the book is structured

Part one

Part one begins by placing ETFs in the context of older forms of collective investments. Chapter 1 shows how the characteristics of ETFs developed from what investment trusts, investment funds (or **unit trusts**) and index tracking had to offer. Core concepts such as benchmarking are explained.

Chapter 2 provides an overview of equity indices – the key to equity ETF differentiation and a cornerstone of the ETF industry.

Chapter 3 looks at the main parties involved in ETF creation and the main types of ETF construction, specifically with reference to equity ETFs (by far the largest type of ETF in terms of assets under management). Familiarity with ETF construction methods is important for understanding the risks involved when investing in ETFs. This thorough examination of ETF construction methods also covers how ETFs handle **discounts** and **premiums** to **net asset value (NAV)**, a key advantage of ETFs in comparison to investment trusts.

Part two

Having looked at the origins of ETFs and how they are created in part one, part two examines the main asset classes that are covered by ETF investing.

Chapter 4 moves on from equity ETFs to look at other asset classes covered by the industry, such as fixed-income and money-market ETFs. Exchange traded products in commodities have a separate section devoted to them (Chapter 5) in order to do justice to the special characteristics of these funds and the indices they track. These asset types are key areas opened up by ETFs and these chapters of the guide are designed to forearm readers with essential information about them.

Chapter 6 then takes a look at some of the more advanced types of exchanged traded fund.

Part three

Part three looks at the practicalities of buying ETFs and how to find out more about individual funds.

In Chapter 7 the practicalities of ETF investing are discussed, including how ETFs can be used by investors, and when and how often ETFs might be traded. Readers may find it helpful to read the 'Searching for an ETF' text box on page 129 early, as this explains how ETF names are constructed.

For many, ETFs present completely new opportunities for acquiring overseas assets so careful thought is given to ETFs and foreign currency considerations in Chapter 8. Attention is also given to the complex area of ETF liquidity.

Chapter 9 draws together conclusions about different types of ETF investment and analyses some broad implications that ETFs have for the investment industry in the future.

* * *

At several points throughout an 'Further reading' section is included. These look at a few of the aspects covered in the preceding pages in more detail. These are not essential for understanding the topics covered in the chapter in which they appear, but may be interesting for some readers.

Note: All ETFs mentioned in the text are indexed with their stock market, or ticker, symbols.

Introduction

What is an ETF?

An exchange traded fund is an investment fund that tracks an index and can be traded like a stock.

This basic definition of an exchange traded fund covers the bare essentials of tracking and tradability, but a slightly longer definition draws out the true nature of ETFs more accurately:

*An ETF is a fund that tracks a basket of **underlying assets** such as an index or a commodity. It is traded on a stock exchange like a security and is designed in such a way as to avoid significant premiums or discounts to the value of the underlying assets.*

ETFs are not actively managed by fund managers selecting assets to buy or sell, and as such they are often referred to as *passive investments*.

Growth of ETFs

In the collective investment industry two trends have stood out in the last ten years. The first is that index tracking funds have continued to grow in favour, at the expense of actively managed funds. The second trend has been the growing popularity of ETFs, firstly in the United States, but increasingly in other parts of the world, not least in Europe.

The progress of ETFs in the 21st century has been impressive. In the United States ETFs and conventional mutual funds that track indices now make up roughly one-sixth of the assets of the fund industry overall. At the end of February 2009 US ETF assets were worth approximately $400bn, while the assets of European domiciled ETFs totalled roughly one-third of this amount. By 2007 new investment coming into tracking funds in the US had already overtaken net inflows into actively managed mutual funds.[1]

---

[1] Eric Rosenbaum, 'Forecast: ETFs to Eclipse Index Funds', IndexUniverse, November 7 2008.

The total number of European ETFs had reached 896 by January 2010 and during the first quarter of 2010 roughly 350 new European ETFs were launched.[2] Figures I.1 and I.2 illustrate the growth of assets under management by European ETFs and the growth in physical numbers of European and London-listed ETFs.

Figure I.1 – The growth of assets under management by European ETFs

Figure I.2 – The growth in the numbers of European and London-listed ETFs

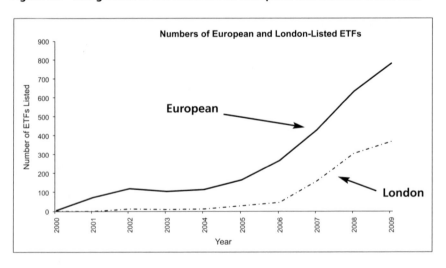

---

[2] Figures from Deutsche Boerse, '10 Years of ETF Trading In Europe'.and IndexUniverse, April 2010.

Although these figures indicate that the number of index tracking ETFs is increasing, there are some complicating factors that mean the analysis of who is buying ETFs is not straightforward – it is not simply the case that retail investors looking for passive investments are making increasing use of ETFs.

Firstly, a large proportion of ETF assets – possibly as high as 60% – are held by professional investors, which suggests that ETFs were not designed with just the interests of retail investors in mind.[3]

Secondly, although ETFs may be overwhelmingly passive tracking instruments, they are used in an active fashion. For example, on the New York Stock Exchange (NYSE) the most popular individual ETFs now have daily share trading volumes that can exceed 5% of the trading volume of the market as a whole. Whereas the turnover of mutual funds was about 33% for the whole of 2008, turnover for exchange traded funds probably exceeds 800% in a year. ETFs were made to be traded; tradability is what attracts professional investors, attracts assets and is the most important reason why providers are interested in sponsoring ETFs in the first place.

This active use of ETFs by professionals is at variance with how ETFs are sometimes thought of. ETFs are positioned as a cheap, versatile adaptation of the mutual fund model of investing, opening up new markets and asset classes to be used as portfolio building blocks but serving primarily as buy-and-hold products (rather than assets to be regularly traded).

A perspective on the different ETF asset classes

While the origins of ETFs undoubtedly lie in equity investing, in the last decade there has been a significant diversification in the kinds of assets that can be tracked by ETFs. The most significant area of growth (after equities) has been in the development of debt and debt security (fixed-income) ETFs (although growth of assets under management for fixed-income ETFs tailed off in the early part of 2010). Figure I.3 illustrates the worldwide growth of assets under management for different ETF classes.

---

[3] Deborah Fuhr, Barclays Global Investors, quoted in an interview with Barron's in June 2009.

Figure I.3 – The worldwide growth of assets under management (AuM) for major ETF asset classes

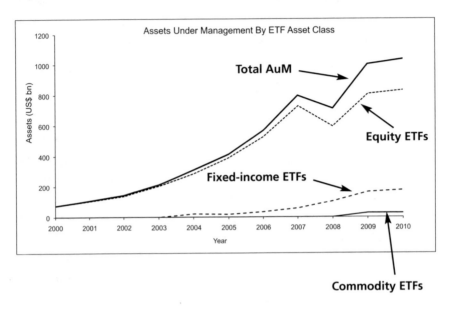

PART ONE:
ETF Basics

Chapter 1
A Short History of Investment Funds

Exchange traded funds are the latest stage in the development of collective investments and they can do more to extend the range of potential investments than anything that preceded them. To gauge the advantages of ETFs it is best to view them in the context of the collective investments that were developed before them, which, in most cases, continue to play a major part in the investment industry, and on which the strengths of ETFs have been built.

The first collective investment

The earliest collective investment vehicle was established in 1774 by a Dutch merchant and stockbroker, Abraham van Ketwich, in the wake of a financial crisis in 1772-3.[4] Van Ketwich's collective investment borrowed its name from the motto of the Dutch Republic, *Eendragt Maakt Magt* (Unity Creates Strength). The *Eendragt Maakt Magt* fund invested not in joint stock companies but instead in a number of collateralised debt securities. These were listed in the prospectus and included lending to the governments of Denmark, Russia, Sweden and various German states and for mortgages on plantations in the Danish, Dutch and British West Indies – a truly international venture.

The novel feature of *Eendragt Maakt Magt* was the stated objective of reducing risk to the investors through diversification. Other features of the investment were, firstly, that it enabled relatively small investors to have access to classes of investment that normally required a substantial commitment of capital and, secondly, it was far more liquid than a direct investment in, say, an individual plantation in the Caribbean. The listing of the target investments meant that the investment was highly inflexible; van Ketwich at this stage was in no way promising to improve investors' returns by means of skilful management. Five

---

[4] K. Geert Rouwenhorst, 'The Origin of Mutual Funds', Yale School of Management – 2003.

years later when van Ketwich introduced his second collective investment he allowed himself far more discretion to alter the investment portfolio and stated that he would be on the lookout for investment opportunities where the price was lower than what he considered to be the intrinsic value. From having just a fiduciary responsibility for his first fund he had turned himself into the world's first fund manager with his second venture.

Both of van Ketwich's funds were **closed end,** signifying that the creation of further shares was not permitted. They were also fixed term, although the lives of both were extended with the consent of investors as the funds were unable to keep to their scheduled redemptions.

The British investment trust phenomenon

Although the first British investment trust, Foreign & Colonial, was established in London in 1868, the wave of investment trusts that appeared in the following 40 years was particularly associated with the cities of Dundee and Edinburgh. The F&C was followed in 1873 by the Scottish American Investment Trust, based in Dundee, which specialised in American railway bonds, and the Scottish American Investment Company (SAINTS), which also started with investments in American railways but soon branched out into the bonds of American states and municipalities, and the US federal government.[5]

Although today we view the typical investment trust as a vehicle for investing in equities, this approach was almost unheard of among British investment trusts until after World War One.[6] Before then British investment trusts confined themselves to bonds and mortgages on overseas properties such as rubber plantations.

---

[5] Although SAINTS is now referred to as an investment trust, at the time it was established there was a distinction between investment trusts and investment companies.

[6] The increase in the proportion of investment trust assets made up of equities had a number of causes. Some equity was acquired through investments in convertible bonds and mortgages. The steep rise in the cost of living during World War One altered investors' attitudes to fixed-interest debt securities. In addition, many of the foreign assets of the investment trusts were compulsorily acquired by the British government in exchange for Treasury stock during the course of the war. In a way British investment trusts had to begin again once the war was over.

In other respects, the investment trusts of the late 19th century and early 20th existed in the form that has continued to the present day. The chief characteristics of investment trusts are as follows:

- Shares in investment trusts are traded on the stock exchange.

- The standard investment trust is *not* fixed-term.[7]

- They are **closed-end** investments – the number of shares is fixed.

- As a consequence of their closed-end nature, investment trust company shares can trade at a premium or a discount to their investments in aggregate. In comparing investment trusts with other collective investment vehicles, these premiums or discounts are a salient feature and can cause difficulty to investors. As we shall see, ETFs and other forms of collective investments have found ways around the problem.[8]

- Capital gains cannot be distributed.

- **Gearing** – adding to a trust's investable funds by borrowing – is permitted.

- Management costs are relatively low – typically under 1% a year.

- Full lists of holdings are only published half yearly.

By 1914 British investment trusts had raised capital totalling approximately £100m (roughly £8.5bn at current values). By 2008 UK investment trusts numbered 450 and had £94bn-worth of assets under management.[9]

The next stage in the development of collective investments, the advent of mutual funds, took place gradually in the United States in the first 40 years of the 20th century.

---

[7] This is a characteristic which distinguishes the ordinary investment trusts from vehicles such as split capital trusts and many venture capital trusts.

[8] Investment trust discounts and premiums to net asset value (NAV) are a still a topic of debate for financial commentators as they add a degree of risk to the investment. As the early investment trusts confined themselves to fixed-term investments, it may not have been of so much concern before 1914.

[9] As at 30 June 2008; source: the Association of Investment Companies.

American investment companies, mutual funds and 1929

The development of mutual funds in the United States was a gradual process of modification of the investment trust model. The latter, which became known as *common trusts* in America, were already becoming popular by the beginning of the 20th century.[10] The first was the Boston Personal Property Trust, founded in 1893.

The first step towards the mutual fund structure was taken with the establishment of the Alexander Fund in Philadelphia in 1907. This introduced two important modifications to the investment trust. Firstly, there were six-monthly issues of new shares, so this was not a **closed-end fund**. Secondly, the fund undertook to redeem (on demand by the investor) its own shares at prices that were close to net asset value (NAV).

Premiums and discounts to net asset value (NAV)

Net asset value (NAV) is the value of the underlying assets of a fund, divided by the number of shares in issue. It is usually expressed as a percentage. A premium or discount to NAV is a situation where there is a discrepancy between the value of the underlying assets in a fund and the value indicated by the share price of the fund. If the share price is higher than the NAV of the fund then the fund is at a premium to NAV and, conversely, if the share price is lower than the NAV then the fund is at a discount to NAV. With an ETF, the NAV is the per share value of the ETF's shares. If the shares of the fund are trading at a lower price than the NAV of the fund then the fund is at a discount to NAV, and vice versa.

The simplest explanation of investment trust premiums and discounts is to recognise that (unlike ETFs) there is no direct relationship between a trust's share price and its NAV – investment trusts normally lack a mechanism for aligning their share price with their asset value. As we will see in Chapter 3, ETFs do have a mechanism for avoiding excessive discounts and premiums to NAV. Indeed, this is one of the key strengths of ETFs.

For more information on discounts to NAV see pages 52 and 60.

---

[10] The US equivalent of an investment trust is now known as a closed-end fund.

Although the Alexander Fund has found a place in history for its innovation, it was neither a trust nor a fund in any legal sense. The fund was simply the investment activities of a banker called W. Wallace Alexander who made investment decisions on behalf of friends and associates. Perhaps it came closest to a modern day share club, with all the investment decisions being taken by one member rather than all. By 1927 Mr Alexander was managing the money of 1700 other people, $4m in total. The Alexander Fund was only wound up in 1941. Although the fund appears to have been run along sound lines, it would not have satisfied the regulatory requirements of the landmark US Investment Company Act of 1940.

The first properly incorporated mutual fund was the Massachusetts Investors Trust (MIT), which was established in 1924. This trust was the first **open-ended fund**; one allowing extra shares to be created to meet investor demand. The trust was also the first to allow share redemptions.[11] All of its portfolio of assets was in the common stock of leading American companies such as General Motors and Eastman Kodak. A further innovation was public disclosure of all its holdings. It was followed a few months later by the State Street Investment Trust, another Boston institution, and the Wellington Fund in Philadelphia in 1928.[12] While MIT aimed to administer its assets conservatively, the Wellington Fund went one step further with the stated objective of a balanced approach to its investment decisions. These aspirations to manage assets in a conservative or balanced fashion can be seen as an early attempt to counteract the dangers of exposure to undue risk.

These fledgling mutual funds were just a sideshow as the 1920s drew to a close. The exciting action at the time was in the new investment trusts such as the Shenandoah Corporation, founded in July 1929, and the Blue Ridge

---

[11] Terminology becomes a little untidy at this point. Mutual fund shares are not the kind that can be traded on a stock exchange. In the UK, reference to the units in a unit trust – the closest UK equivalent – was a useful distinction.

[12] The Wellington Fund started out life as the Industrial and Power Securities Company. The fund managers made the happy decision to sell a lot of their equity portfolio before the crash of autumn of 1929. The name was changed because the word 'industrial' was believed to have gone out of fashion after the crash. ('Reflections on Wellington Fund's 75th Birthday', Bogle Financial Markets Research Centre.)

Corporation, founded the following month. American investment trusts in the late 1920s were the primary symptom of the speculative mania of the time, with assets rising from roughly $720m at the start of 1927 to $8bn by September 1929.[13] The (mainly) new investment trusts' shares were trading at substantial premiums to their asset values, many were investing in the shares of other investment trusts and many were highly leveraged. Added to that, high fees were charged by the trusts' promoters, and brokers' commissions were also high. When the Wall Street Crash came the American version of the investment trust model went into decline.

Disillusionment with the investment trust structure was the moment of opportunity for the as yet small scale mutual fund movement, known in the 1930s as the Boston-type trust.[14] Of course, the mutual funds, of which there were 19 in 1929, did not escape the crash unscathed – MIT shares reached a peak of $65 in 1929 and had sunk as low as $11 by 1932 – but at least they were still in business. When M&G launched the first British unit trust in 1931 it was deliberately emulating the US mutual fund model.[15]

The main characteristics of mutual funds/unit trusts are as follows:

- Although not tradable securities in their own right, purchase and sale of units is straightforward. Buying direct from the fund manager is normally more expensive than buying through a broker, however.

- The price for unit trusts is set once a day.

- Unit trusts are **open-ended investments** so the number of units grows when new investors commit funds and shrinks when existing unit holders cash in their investments.

---

[13] J. K. Galbraith, *The Great Crash 1929*.

[14] 'Boston Trusts', *Time* magazine, 5 October 1936.

[15] The first M&G trust was in fact a fixed trust with a 20-year lifespan. When this expired in 1951 it was succeeded by the M&G General Trust Fund.

- There is a significant difference between the bid and offer price of units in a unit trust. Normally this is about 6-7%, but unit trusts can increase the spread to 10% in periods of volatility. This is known as 'moving to bid basis'.[16]

- Investors cashing in their units in large numbers can have a significant impact on the share market. Unlike investment trusts, unit trust managers will have to sell part of their portfolio.

- Financial advisers and other brokers may impose substantial initial charges for selling unit trusts (although commission on purchasing some other investment products is even higher). The amount of the initial charge can be in the region of 5%. Although this charge is a one-off, it represents a significant amount of ground to be made up before the investment returns a profit.

- Management charges are at 1-2% a year, which is somewhat higher than for investment trusts.

- Unit trusts normally pay a dividend twice a year and issue annual and half-yearly reports.

- UK unit trusts do not pay capital gains tax on any capital gains they realise (although, of course, investors may be liable for capital gains tax when they cash in their holdings).

- Unit trusts are not allowed gearing.

Unit trusts ruling the roost

The first of the UK-based overseas funds – the M&G Japan and General Fund – was launched in 1971. Today there are unit trusts specialising in virtually every region of the world and in many different kinds of investment. By the end of 2007 the value of assets managed by UK-domiciled funds like unit trusts had risen to £468bn.[17]

---

[16] Open ended investment companies (OEICs) must operate with single pricing, that is with no difference between the bid or buying price and the offer or selling price. In recent years many unit trusts have converted themselves into OEICs. See the section on OEICs in 'Other types of fund' on page 23.

[17] The Investment Management Association.

In the United States the move towards mutual funds has been even more impressive. By 2005 there was $8905bn under management by mutual funds and over 47% of US households had mutual fund investments.[18] It was in the United States that the next major refinement of collective investments, and the next step towards ETFs, took place – the advent of passive or tracker funds.

The advent of tracker funds

The first tracker fund was established at the end of 1975 by John Bogle in the form of the Index Investment Trust.[19] The clue was in the name; it had the apparently simple aim of tracking an index. The rationale behind this was that actively managed funds do not consistently outperform the market – an insight supported by the **efficient market hypothesis (EMH)**. Not only that, actively managed funds necessarily generate high transaction costs. Therefore, Bogle decided to track indices and match their returns rather than trying to outperform them.

At the time the notion was scorned as not being ambitious enough to suit investors but now the attraction of a fund investment performing no worse than its benchmark is much better appreciated.

The first British retail tracker funds did not appear until almost 20 years after their American counterparts. Although tracker funds were popular in the UK in the 1990s, the total amount under management in tracker funds has failed to reach the scale of conventional unit trusts.[20] Tracker funds had a total of £24.5bn at the end of the first quarter of 2008, compared to £26.3bn a year earlier.[21]

---

[18] Mellon Global Investments quoting the Investment Company Institute. In fact the figures for the number of US households investing in mutual funds had peaked the previous year in absolute terms and as a proportion of the total number of households.

[19] The name was later changed to the Vanguard 500 Index Fund. Bogle already had years of experience with the Wellington funds including the period in the late 1960s and early 1970s when their performance had deteriorated. In fact, his fund can only claim the place of first *retail* index fund; index funds had been set up for institutional clients of two US banks a couple of years earlier.

[20] Of course, the phrase 'under management' is somewhat misleading in this context but it continues to be used. Commentators on the exchange traded fund scene also speak of 'funds under management'.

[21] The Investment Management Association.

The main characteristics of tracker funds are as follows:

- There are no initial charges for buying.

- Management charges are significantly lower; normally not more than 1% and possibly as low as 0.3%. (The fund manager will be spending a lot less on researching the portfolio so this is only fair.)

- Tracker funds can be bought and sold in just the same way as ordinary investment funds.

- Relative to active funds, tracker funds are few in number. Of these a proportion are provided by banks and marketed exclusively through their own distribution channels.

- Like other unit trusts, tracker prices are set once a day; it is not possible to react speedily to threats or opportunities in the index being tracked.

- Stock exchange indices work in ideal conditions with, for instance, no broker's commission to pay when a stock joins the index. The tracker fund exists in the real world and there are small costs to the tracking process. This is one instance of **tracking error**, a term we shall be encountering again in the context of exchange traded funds.[22]

Closet trackers

In addition to investment funds that track stock market indices overtly, there is a considerable amount of unacknowledged tracking going on across the investment fund industry. Funds that in practice effectively just track an index, despite marketing themselves as being actively managed, are known as *closet trackers* and have attracted considerable criticism, mainly on the grounds that they are not working hard enough to justify their management fees.

Of course, highly respected fund managers leading substantial research teams may use tracking strategies on occasion. Tracking with part of a portfolio can be a worthwhile strategy just like keeping some cash uninvested. However, for actively managed funds using, say, the FTSE 100 as a benchmark, there has been a tendency for fund managers to include all the index constituents but with smaller holdings of the companies that they expect to perform poorly.

---

[22] 'Tracking error' is a phrase that is put to different uses by different commentators. The Glossary gives an explanation of the main ways in which the term is used.

In this way the managers cover themselves in case the less favoured stocks surprise with a better performance than expected.

European Union regulation (UCITS)

Before bringing this brief overview up to date with exchange traded funds it is worthwhile taking a look at the effect of European Union law on collective investments because this is definitive for the form of individual ETFs in the EU, and the overall marketplace for investing. As we shall see later, UCITS (undertakings for collective investment in transferable securities) explains some significant differences between European ETFs and their American counterparts.

UCITS is the name of a series of EU directives that aim to make it possible for securities to be marketed throughout the EU even though they have only been authorised in a single member state.[23] It could be described as a passport for investment funds. This principle has taken a long time to put into effect and the process is not yet complete.

The latest directive, UCITS III,[24] introduced a number of changes which directly impact on ETFs (and older types of collective investments):

1. A distinction was made between unsophisticated investment vehicles, such as traditional mutual funds, and sophisticated ones, which included ETFs and funds investing in derivatives or using hedging techniques such as shorting.

---

[23] Collective investments that are not UCITS' compliant are known as 'nurs' (non-UCITS retail scheme) and are only permitted to be sold in the country in which they were authorised (under the country's national regulatory regime). UCITS' compliant funds accounted for about 70% of the total funds market in the EU at the end of 2005 although the totals varied between individual member states (for example: Spain – almost 100% of funds; Republic of Ireland – about 80% of funds in 2007; Austria – about 65% of funds).

[24] UCITS lll was adopted by the EU in 2001 but only became binding in February 2007. UCITS lV is due to come into effect in 2011 and will bring about significant curtailment of the scrutiny UCITS' compliant investments can be subjected to by national regulators before they can be sold to the public. The amount of documentation that is required to be translated into local languages will also be reduced. UCITS' standards are well respected and commentators will often refer to them for purposes of comparison with regulations in other jurisdictions, especially in cases where these regulations are older or less rigorous.

2. UCITS III-compliant vehicles must provide access to a simplified prospectus that gives clear information about the risks that investing in that vehicle will expose one to.

3. No single security may exceed 10% of a UCITS NAV while the total number of holdings exceeding 5% of the UCITS NAV may not cumulatively exceed 40% of NAV. This is the so-called **5/10/40 rule.**

4. UCITS' compliant investments are limited to 20% exposure to a single group of funds.

5. Investors in unsophisticated funds should not be exposed to a loss greater than the amount paid for the investment. Sophisticated funds are permitted leverage of up to 200% of their net asset value.

6. Regular, accurate and comprehensive information on a fund's portfolio has to be available.

7. Investments have to be relatively liquid and negotiable.[25]

8. Effective measurement of the risk of the securities invested in has to be undertaken.

9. A fund may not be exposed to a **counterparty risk** that is equal to more than 10% of the net asset value where the counterparty is a bank or otherwise 5%.

Several aspects of UCITS III, particularly requirements relating to liquidity, portfolio information and maximum counterparty risks, are hot topics as far as the workings of European ETFs are concerned. However, to tell the story of ETFs from the beginning we have to look back to North America.

---

[25] A typical example of a vehicle non-compliant in this respect might be a real estate investment trust (REIT) where the manager reserves the right to limit or suspend redemptions.

The first exchange traded funds

By general consensus the first investment vehicles approximating to the ETFs of today were the Toronto Index Participation Units (TIPS[26]) launched on 9 March 1990. The TIPS combined the index tracking, low management cost and tax benefits features that have become hallmarks of ETFs. The particular index tracked by TIPS was the Toronto Stock Exchange 35, the main index for large cap Canadian companies.

In fact, TIPS were not the first index participation units. The previous year had seen an attempt by the American Stock Exchange (AMEX) and Philadelphia Stock Exchange (PHLX) to introduce very similar instruments. However, these index participation units fell foul of a regulators' turf war when the Commodity Futures Trading Commission (CFTC) contested the authorisation they had been granted by the Securities and Exchange Commission (SEC) on the grounds that the instruments were futures not securities. The federal courts upheld this objection and the exchanges ceased trading them.

Today, TIPS' claim to primacy has been overshadowed by the oldest surviving ETF,[27] the Standard & Poors 500 Depositary Receipt (known as Spider and normally abbreviated as **SPDR** Index 500).[28] Established in 1993 with a subsidiary of the American Exchange as its **sponsor** and the State Street Bank and Trust as **trustee**, SPDR Index 500 is also the world's largest ETF with assets worth $94bn at the end of 2008.

---

[26] Not to be confused with Treasury Inflation Protected Securities in the US, which are also known as TIPS.

[27] TIPS and HIPS (which tracked the Toronto Stock Exchange 100 Share Index) were phased out in early 2001 and replaced with i60 units that tracked the new Standard & Poors/TSE 60 Index.

[28] Not all depositary receipts are ETFs. They can also be a device to enable investors to avail themselves of overseas investment opportunities in single companies while still enjoying the regulatory protection of their domestic stock exchange. For example, USA investors in Vodafone may purchase Vodafone American Depositary Receipts (ADRs) on the New York Stock Exchange. Normally, an ADR will bundle a small number of the company's shares together. Clearly, ETFs take the bundling process to far greater lengths but, in a sense, the principle is the same.

The logic behind passive investing and ETFs

Academic research has found that investors cannot beat the market consistently by picking stocks themselves – in other words, *active investing is not successful in the long term*. Evidence for this comes from a statistical analysis of historical performance and it is explained by the efficient market hypothesis.

Therefore passive investing – investing in a fund that tracks the performance of an index – is a sensible strategy.

ETFs incorporate the best of the investment vehicles that went before them

A helpful way to view exchange traded funds is to see them as a hybrid combining some of the most useful features of the types of collective investment vehicles that have gone before:

- *Investment trusts* – ETFs have the advantage of the tradability that investment trusts enjoy through having a stock exchange listing; they can be traded all the time that the stock market is open for business.[29] ETFs publish their holdings on a daily basis compared to the twice-yearly or quarterly publication of holdings for investment trusts and closed-end funds.

- *Mutual funds/unit trusts* – unlike investment trusts, ETFs have the advantage of avoiding large discounts or premiums to net asset value, just as the mutual funds do. Like mutual funds. ETFs have the ability to create or cancel their own shares in response to investor demand.

---

[29] One drawback that investment trusts and ETFs have is that their method of purchase (via a stock exchange) makes **cost averaging** uneconomic.

- *Tracker funds* – ETFs offer the risk-reducing advantages of trackers in that they should perform no worse than their benchmark index. ETFs also share tracker funds' attractive low expenses. Unlike trackers and other mutual funds, ETFs are fully invested at all times; no cash has to be kept in hand to fund redemptions.[30]

In Chapter 3 the mechanics of ETF creation will be looked at in more detail to see the ways in which one form of investment can incorporate all these advantages at the same time.

The key qualities of ETFs

- low expense ratios

- simplicity (relative to other investments)

- transparency (being able to see the investment that underlies the ETF)

- good liquidity and low bid/offer spreads

- reduction of risk by tracking broad indices

- reduction of risk by investing across different markets

- low **tracking difference**

- a degree of regulatory protection. [31]

---

[30] Although they may have dividends awaiting distribution to their shareholders.

[31] In addition to this list of attractions is the fundamental advantage of being exchange-traded, but in the context of advanced ETFs this ease of access may be a dangerous thing.

The expansion of ETFs in Europe

Before looking at how the spread of ETFs that are on offer to European investors has grown, three important points deserve prior consideration:

1. It is important to keep in mind the distinction between the market where an ETF can be bought, the jurisdiction under which it is operated and the market that the ETF invests in. For example, one may be able to buy an ETF on the London Stock Exchange which is domiciled in Ireland and invests in the United States.

2. There has been a broad trend of ETFs becoming more specialised. To put this another way, ETF sponsors started with ETFs that targeted obvious stock indices (such as the FTSE 100 and the S&P 500) and, generally speaking, have moved into areas that are less obvious. For example, in the US there are now not only ETFs tracking the healthcare sector as a whole but ones tracking treatments for specific kinds of illness.

3. The various ETF sponsors sometimes compete with similar ETFs covering the same index. This is particularly true in the case of the more well-known indices.[32] However, directly competing ETFs are not numerous; if examined closely more often than not two similar ETFs will have more to distinguish them than merely different management fees.

---

[32] As of June 2008 there were 13 different ETFs licensed to track the DJ Euro STOXX 50 but multiple index licensing – competing funds tracking the same index – is much less common in the United States. However, Deutsche Bank Research forecast that this would change. (EU Monitor 55, Deustche Bank Research.)

The European ETF industry: the first ten years

The first European-domiciled ETFs appeared in 2000. Merrill Lynch was the first on the scene with its Dow Jones Euro STOXX 50 and Dow Jones STOXX 50 LDRS ETFs, which were listed on the Deutsche Boerse.[33] They were quickly followed by the iShares FTSE 100 ETF.

The first ETF to track the main French stock index, the CAC 40, was launched on the Euronext Paris market the following year by Société Générale[34] and went by the name CAC 40 Master Unit. In May of that year SG launched the Dow Jones Master Unit, which tracked the Dow Jones Industrial Average (DJIA).

When is an ETF European?

With the strong possibility that an ETF's domicile, exchange and index could each be in a different country, describing ETFs is a tricky business. To a European, a European ETF probably means one that is domiciled in a European country and traded on a European exchange (and hence regulated by a European regulator). In the United States a European ETF will probably refer to one tracking a European index.

To avoid ambiguity, it is probably best to describe ETFs that residents of European countries can (easily) trade as European-domiciled.

In the context of the names of ETFs, *euro* invariably refers to one tracking an index in the euro currency area and *Europe* can appear as an element in the names of ETFs tracking an index of European companies inside and outside the euro-area, including countries outside the EU altogether.

---

[33] LDRS, which stands for 'leaders', was Merrill Lynch's branding for these ETFs. Their sponsorship was transferred from Merrill Lynch to iShares in September 2003 and their names were changed to iShares DJ STOXX 50 and iShares DJ EURO STOXX 50. As one would expect, the latter tracks an index of companies in eight countries in the euro zone. Less obviously, the iShares DJ STOXX 50 tracks an index of companies in 17 European countries. Index publishers and ETF sponsors often demonstrate a surprising faith in the potency of their brands.

[34] The Société Générale **master units** are now sold under the Lyxor brand.

The first European-domiciled ETF to track a global index was the EasyETF Global Titans 50 Fund. The Global Titans 50 index is another Dow Jones index and it covers the stocks of very large companies that have (some) operations outside their home country.

In 2003 iShares launched Europe's first corporate bond ETF, the iBOXX[35] Liquid Corporates ETF.[36] The first ETF tracking the S&P 500 for European investors was also launched by iShares. By 2004 there were some 120 European-domiciled ETFs with assets of €25bn.

The first European-domiciled ETF to track dividend-weighted indices were Indexchange's[37] DJ Euro STOXX Select Dividend 30 and DJ STOXX Select Dividend 30 ETFs, which were launched in 2005, the year that saw European-domiciled ETFs and their assets really take off. In the same year EasyETF also achieved a first with the launch of the S&P GSCI (Goldman Sachs Commodities Index) ETF. The following year XACT Fonder[38] launched the first ETF to track a fundamentally weighted index, the XACT FTSE RAFI (Research Affiliates Fundamental Index) Fundamental Euro ETF.

By the beginning of 2009, the number of European-domiciled ETFs had grown to over 600 and their combined assets totalled in the region of €150bn. This compares with $535bn-worth of assets for US-based ETFs at the end of 2008. At the time of writing, no less than one-quarter of (European-domiciled) ETFs were launched in 2008 alone.

Listings of ETFs available to European investors are now easily obtainable in print and online,[39] and online sharedealing services that double as mutual fund supermarkets are beginning to pay more attention to the demand for ETFs.

---

[35] iBOXX was originally a consortium of seven European banks and specialised in publishing indices for fixed interest securities. The brand is now owned by Markit, itself a privately held company with 16 banking shareholders.

[36] The name is now iShares € Corporate Bond ETF.

[37] Indexchange was acquired by Barclays Global Investors from Bayerische Hypo-und Vereinsbank (HVB) in November 2006. Alhough no longer an ETF sponsor, HVB remains important in the field through its activities as an ETF swap counterparty, market-maker and custodian.

[38] The leading ETF sponsor in the Nordic region, part of Svenska Handelsbanken.

[39] *Money Observer*, for example, began listing prices for leading European-domiciled ETFs in August 2008.

Table 1.1 – The top 20 ETFs on the LSE by trading volume

Name	EPIC	100-day average turnover[40]	Assets held (£m)[41]
iShares FTSE 100	ISF	42,913,500	3,350
Lyxor Gold Bullion Securities Ltd	GBS	16,104,044	2,590
ETFS Physical Gold	PHAU	8,248,425	2,180
iShares iBoxx £ Corporate Bond	SLXX	8,091,630	1,110
iShares S&P 500 (sterling)	IUSA	7,264,500	4,210
ETFS Natural Gas	NGAS	5,694,590	470
ETFS Leveraged Crude Oil	LOIL	5,560,381	100
iShares FTSE 250	MIDD	5,094,530	300
iShares S&P 500 (dollar)	IDUS	5,080,283	4,130
iShare DJ Euro STOXX 50	EUE	4,621,300	3,410
iShares MSCI Emerging Markets	IEEM	3,872,975	1,970
iShares GBP Index Linked Gilt	INXG	3,833,220	500
ETFS Crude Oil	CRUD	3,671,067	240
iShares FTSE UK Gilt All Stocks	IGLT	3,592,540	300
iShares MSCI AC Far East ex-Japan	IFFF	3,425,500	1,680
ETFS Short Crude Oil	SOIL	3,389,752	60
IShares MSCI World	IWRD	3,226,810	1,800
ETFS Brent 1 Month Oil Securities	OILB	2,999,702	180
iShares Euro Corporate Bond	IBCX	2,796,768	2,920
iShares MSCI Japan	IJPN	2,766,885	1,170

[40] Over 100 days to 10 February 2010.

[41] These asset figures for mid-February 2010 are approximate (to the nearest £10 million); bear in mind that the actual assets of many of these ETFs are in euro or dollars. Note that soft commodity ETFs in general and leveraged or short ones in particular have a much higher ratio of turnover to assets than equity or fixed-income ETFs.

Further reading

Other types of fund

OEICs

Open-ended investment companies (OEICs) combine some of the features of an investment trust and an investment fund. In the UK they have only been in existence since 1997 but they have a much longer history in the rest of Europe. The Dutch active fund manager, Robeco, has been a pioneer of this type of structure since the end of the 1920s.

OEICs avoid discounts or premiums to net asset value because as open-ended entities they can simply issue more shares in line with investor demand and investors can sell their shares back to the company instead of having to trade them on the stock market. In this they are more like investment funds. However, unlike investment funds, investors do not encounter bid/offer spreads when investing or cashing in their investment. This simplifies matters enormously and is one of the main attractions of OEICs. In continental Europe single pricing is a requirement for investment funds so UK unit trust managers have had important incentives for converting unit trusts into OEICs.

(Irish) variable capital companies

Variable capital companies are another hybrid of investment trusts – in that they are companies – and investment funds. The market capitalisation of the issued shares must be equal to the net asset value of the underlying assets at all times, and this balance is maintained by the companies' ability to purchase their own shares.

The main difference between an Irish variable capital company[42] and a British OEIC is that the former will have a stock market quote. This means that they meet the legal requirements in some countries where institutional investors are only able to invest in quoted instruments.

---

[42] Many other European countries have variable capital companies as well as Ireland.

XTF: a dedicated market for ETFs

Deutsche Boerse demonstrated considerable foresight in establishing the dedicated **XTF** market for trading in tracking products such as ETFs as long ago as 2000. At roughly the same time moves were in hand to introduce euro-denominated trading in US equities on its Xetra platform. It was believed that the volume of US equities being traded would assist in the creation and redemption process for ETFs tracking US equities and being traded on XTF.

By September 2003 XTF accounted for 55% of trading in ETFs on European exchanges, compared to just 4.9% for the London Stock Exchange's **extraMARK** platform. For the third quarter of 2008 XTF's share of the market had dropped to 39% but it remained ahead of its nearest rivals: NextTrack (with a 26% share), Borsa Italiana (with 16%) and LSE (with 10%). extraMARK is no longer used as a separate market segment).

Chapter 2

The Role of Indices

By their very nature ETFs need to track an index and so it is no coincidence that the proliferation in the number of ETFs in recent years has been accompanied by a similar growth in the numbers and types of indices.

This crucial role of indices can be seen just by looking at the names of ETFs themselves, for instance, SPDR Index 500, Lyxor ETF FTSE 250 and iShares DJ STOXX 600 Technology ETF, all of which include the title of the index they track in their name. In the last ten years, the development of ETFs and that of indices has become so closely related that some indices have come into existence purely designed to be tracked by ETFs.[43]

Considering the importance of indices in how ETFs operate, it is clear that in order to understand an ETF it is essential to understand the index it tracks. With this in mind, we will now move on to look at different methods of index construction.

---

[43] The mutual dependence of funds and indices extends to traditional mutual funds as well as ETFs. This was recognised in 2001 in a landmark case between Vanguard and S&P. Standard & Poors took Vanguard to court because they weren't happy that the latter was only paying $50,000 a year for a licence to include '500' in the name of its flagship Vanguard 500 Index Fund (The, McGraw Hill Companies. Inc v. Vanguard Index Trust & The Vanguard Group, Inc., US District Court of the Southern District of New York). Vanguard was blocked from pegging new products to the S&P 500 Index and was unable to introduce a **VIPER** ETF to track the S&P 500 the following year. Instead the VIPER ETFs tracked Wilshire 5000 and 4500 indices. Since then the interdependence of stock indices and ETFs has been more widely appreciated.

Methods of index calculation

Indices can be calculated in a number of different ways. In this section we will look at the following five methods:

1. capitalisation-weighted indices

2. style and **segment indices**

3. fundamentally weighted indices

4. equally weighted indices

5. **price-weighted** indices

1. Capitalisation-weighted indices

The most important characteristic of some of the better-known stock indices is their use of market capitalisation to weight their constituents. This process means that the greater a company's market capitalisation, the more influence any movement in its price will have over the value of the index as a whole. Using market capitalisation (cap-weighting) elegantly solves the two main problems of index design simultaneously: firstly, which stocks to include in the index and, secondly, the weighting to give the constituent stocks once they have qualified to be included. Yet, market capitalisation has a relatively short history; the S&P 500 only dates back to 1957 and the FTSE 100 is younger still, dating from 1984.

The construction of a cap-weighted index

Let us consider an ETF based on a notional index of UK water companies. The weightings of the four companies in our notional index are based on the cap-weighted method of index construction. The following table shows how that index is constructed.[44]

---

[44] The figures used in this example are purely for purposes of illustration and only approximate to actual share prices for these companies in the latter part of 2009.

Table 2.1 – Cap-weighted method of index construction for water companies

Index constituents	Price (pence)	No. of shares outstanding (m)	Market capitalisation (£bn)	Index (& ETF) weighting
Northumbrian Water	250	520	1.3	14.7%
Pennon	500	350	1.75	19.8%
Severn Trent	1000	240	2.4	27.1%
United Utilities	500	680	3.4	38.4%

In recent years index theorists have suggested that there may be better ways to design indices than cap-weighting. Once tracking funds appeared and theories about tracking indices began to be studied carefully, the idea that cap-weighted indices could be used to reckon the health of the whole stock market was bound to be examined more closely.

Broadly speaking, investors only began to question the wisdom of tracking cap-weighted indices after the bursting of the dotcom bubble in 2000 because investors realised that cap-weighting had caused them to be overweight in technology stocks. By late 1999 the S&P 500 was up approximately 15% on the level at the start of the year, not an extraordinary improvement, but nearly all of the growth was in the index's high tech sector; the prices of many non-tech stocks on the index were falling.

An example of the problems that can be caused by over-weighting with cap-weighted indices – drawn from the dotcom crash – is provided by the Powershares QQQ ETF. This ETF launched in March 1999 and tracks the NASDAQ 100 (the top non-financial stocks quoted on NASDAQ), which is also based on market capitalisation. It suffered falls of 37% in 2000 and 31% in 2001 because it was so heavily weighted to tech stocks.

A straightforward alternative to a cap-weighted index is an index where all the stocks in the index receive equal-weighting by value irrespective of any other factor. In the case of the notional index of UK water companies used as an example above, each company would have a 25% weighting in the index. The rationale for equally weighted indices is explained later in this chapter.

2. Style and segment indices: an early alternative to cap-weighting

An alternative to cap-weighted indices has been available since the 1980s in the form of style indices. However, these were designed as benchmarks for the (actively managed) mutual funds industry.

The inspiration for style indices, which are indices based on growth or value criteria, was the debate about the relative advantages of growth and value approaches to investing. Growth enthusiasts look at a stock's potential for growth while advocates of value investing look for stocks that are priced at less than their intrinsic value suggests they are worth. When index tracking funds such as ETFs emerged the idea of style ETFs presented itself as an obvious alternative to funds tracking cap-weighted indices.

Definitions of style

Growth – a growth company is one whose earnings and/or revenue are growing faster than average for its industry sector or the stock market as whole.

Value – a value stock is one where the company's share price is low relative to the dividend (so dividend yield is high) and the earnings (so the price-earnings ratio is high).

Russell style indices – these use a combination of the ratio of the **book value** to price and the stock's long-term growth mean according to the Institutional Brokers Estimate System (IBES), a compilation of growth estimates by stock analysts.

Dow Jones Wilshire style indices – a combination of the following: IBES long-term growth forecasts, price to (future) earnings ratio based on IBES one-year forecasts, price to book ratio, dividend yield, the previous five years' revenue growth and earnings growth for the previous 21 quarters.

S&P style indices – have their own ways of measuring for growth and value. The following three measures of growth are used: five-year earnings per share growth, five-year revenue per share growth and five-

---

year internal growth rate.[45] Value is measured by price to book value ratio, price to cash flow ratio, price to sales ratio and dividend yield. S&P also have **pure style indices**, where the weighting as well as the stock selection depends on style measurements.

MSCI (formerly Morgan Stanley Capital Index)/Barra style indices – Like S&P, different measures are used for growth and value.

The first firm to develop style indices was the Californian company Wilshire, which launched its flagship Dow Jones Wilshire 5000 Total Market Index in 1974/5.[46] The company's growth and value style indices, which went under the name 'Target Indexes', were launched in 1986.[47] In March 2009 Dow Jones and Wilshire went separate ways meaning that Dow Jones' Total Stock Market indices and Wilshire Associates' indices are now independent of each other.

The year after the Target Indexes were launched, Frank Russell Associates introduced its version of growth and value indices. In 1984 the company had already pioneered its Russell 1000 large cap index and the Russell 2000 small cap index, benchmarks that would provide an improved measure of the kinds of strategies that mutual fund investment managers were following. Together with the mid cap index, these are normally referred to as **segment indices**. Russell growth and value indices (and segment indices) are tracked by a number of iShares ETFs.[48] Rydex Investments also has ETFs and mutual funds that track Russell segment indices.

---

[45] Internal growth rate is defined as return on equity (ROE) x earnings retention rate.

[46] The Dow Jones Wilshire 5000 actually comprises 6700 constituents and is the United States' broadest equity index. It is tracked by the Vanguard Total Stock Market VIPER.

[47] The Target Indexes lasted until 2006 when they were replaced by a new range of growth and value indices in partnership with Dow Jones.

[48] In 1999 George Keane, then trustee of the New York Common Retirement Fund proposed switching half of the fund's assets from tracking the S&P 500 to tracking the Russell 1000 Value Index instead. His suggestion was opposed and the fund was still fully exposed to the S&P 500 when the tech bubble burst. However, Research Affiliates consulted with George Keane extensively in developing their alternative approach to cap-weighted indices.

The rationale for tracking different stock market styles and segments is the belief that they will show a *forecastable* variation in performance from that of the market as a whole. Which styles and segments will outperform the market may vary with time and is often hotly debated, but there is no doubt of the utility of funds that track different styles and segments.

Value style indices serve a useful purpose as a benchmark for funds that are aiming to reduce risk and the volatility of returns. More surprisingly, value indices have demonstrated a long-term ability to outperform growth ones.[49] However, as described in the 'Definitions of style' box on pages 30-31, there is no unanimity as to what constitutes value when it comes to index design.

One advantage of style (and fundamentally weighted) indices, and the ETFs that track them, is that a general idea of the weighting process can be obtained without requiring the investment of time in calculating share ratios and reading company accounts that would be required to put into effect such a strategy if selecting individual stocks. Thus, ETFs offer an attractive combination of benefiting from others' expertise without having to yield control over one's investment decisions.

3. Fundamentally weighted indices

The exponents of fundamental weighting believe that the indices they design are better for tracking than cap-weighted indices. However, the claims made for fundamentally weighted indices remain deeply controversial in the eyes of many advocates of cap-weighting.

---

[49] Recently, it has been argued that a growth style index with the weighting based on fundamentals would overcome this disadvantage and that WisdomTree's Largecap Growth Fund (USA constituents weighted by earnings) and International Largecap Growth Fund (non-USA constituents weighted by dividends) do just this. (Luciano Siracusano, 'Fundamentally Weighted Growth Indexes', Index Universe, 26 December 2008.)

The fundamental index method

One of the strongest cases against cap-weighting was led by Robert Arnott and Jason Hsu of Research Affiliates, who developed (and trademarked) the fundamental index method. Their basic insight is that investors in a cap-weighted index like the S&P 500 will be overweight in overvalued stocks and underweight in undervalued ones. In the three to four years following the bursting of the tech bubble they developed and tested an alternative to cap-weighting based on performance under four fundamental criteria: sales, cash flow, dividends and book value.

Research Affiliates gave equal weighting to each of its four measures to produce a composite figure for each company that was an average of these metrics.[50] Their research showed that in the period from 1962 to 2004 a fundamentally weighted index such as theirs would have outperformed the S&P 500 by an average of roughly 2% a year.

The company's indices go under the name RAFI (Research Affiliates Fundamental Index) and the company states that $38bn of assets are managed using strategies it has developed. The company publishes indices in partnership with FTSE, and its fundamental indices are used by ETF sponsors such as Claymore, Lyxor and Powershares as well as tracker fund managers such as Charles Schwab. You can tell if an ETF is tracking a Research Affiliates Fundamental Index by the use of RAFI or fundamental index in the name, as in Powershares FTSE RAFI Europe Fund, which tracks the 1000-constituent FTSE RAFI Europe Index.

[Readers are advised to look at Research Affiliates' own material to find out about their approach as index publishers and commentators have struggled to do justice to the debate over index weighting.]

---

[50] In the case of those companies that don't pay dividends the composite was the average of the other three fundamentals, which gives these companies an edge (in the weighting) over companies that only pay small dividends.

The debate over cap-weighted and fundamentally weighted indices

The respective advantages of cap-weighting and fundamental-weighting continue to be debated.

Cap-weighting does have arguments in its favour. The efficient market hypothesis, the theory behind the idea that most investors who select individual stocks will not beat the market most of the time, helps to underpin both tracking in general and tracking cap-weighted indices in particular. If it is thought that the market is pricing shares efficiently, it makes sense to use the indexing method that combines pricing with numbers of shares, thus market cap-weighting. Some advocates of cap-weighting even dispute whether a fundamentally weighted index is truly an index and whether an ETF tracking it can be truly described as passive (because a lot of selection criteria have gone into the construction of the index).

Weighting by dividend or dividend yield

A variation on the fundamental index theme is the weighting of an index by dividend or dividend yield. Indices thus weighted include the Dow Jones US Select Dividend Index (tracked by iShares Dow Jones US Select Dividend ETF) and WisdomTree Investments Indexes.[51] WisdomTree also manages earnings-weighted indices and ETFs that track them.

4. Equally-weighted indices

The typical equally weighted index will use market capitalisation to select the index constituents but not to decide the proportion of the index that is allocated to each particular constituent. The effect (and purpose) of equal weighting is to neutralise the tendency of cap-weighting to make an index overweight in overvalued stocks and underweight in undervalued ones.

---

[51] WisdomTree is unusual in being both an index publisher and an ETF sponsor. However, WisdomTree Investments, the index publisher, and the WisdomTree Trust, the ETF manager/sponsor, are separate entities.

The very first tracking strategy, designed by the Wells Fargo Bank for the Samsonite pension fund in 1971, was one that used equal weighting. The first mutual fund to use equal weighting was the Morgan Stanley Value-Added Market Equity Fund established in 1987 and the first equally weighted ETF was the Rydex S&P Equal Weight Fund in 2003. The indices used by the Rydex S&P Equal Weight ETF and Rydex's sector equal-weight ETFs[52] are designed and operated by S&P rather than merely being adaptations of S&P's cap-weighted indices.

Equal weighting illustrates a serious disadvantage of all non-cap-weighted indices; as a method of maintaining indices non-cap-weighting seems more arbitrary and more artificial than other methods of weighting. An index is supposed to track the price changes of its constituents, so one that stayed equally weighted all the time would be a contradiction. In fact, equally weighted indices are only truly equally weighted on the day they are rebalanced. In the case of S&P's equally weighted indices this is done quarterly.

Thus, the chief characteristic of an ETF following an equally weighted index is not tracking in its pure form but automatic portfolio rebalancing. Similarly, a fundamentally weighted index, for example, is also characterised by routine rebalancing in order to reset it according to its original fundamental criteria.

The rebalancing required for an equal-weight fund or fundamentally weighted fund can add significantly to the expense of the fund. This is because the fund manager will need to make sales or purchases of every stock in the index to rebalance it, instead of simply having to buy the stock of new constituents and sell that of companies that have been demoted from the index as happens with funds tracking cap-weighted indices. Wells Fargo gave up on equal weighting for the Samsonite pension fund after a few years for this reason. The dealing costs of rebalancing were adversely affecting the fund's net returns.

---

[52] Launched in 2006.

Table 2.2 looks at how quarterly rebalancing would work in relation to our notional index of equally weighted water companies.

Table 2.2 – How quarterly rebalancing works in practice

Index constituents	Price (pence)	Weighting by value in index at start of the quarter	Number of each company's shares in an initial £10,000 invested in tracking the index	Change in share price over the quarter	Weighting by value in index at the end of the quarter (overall the index has dropped by 5%)	Sale/purchase of shares needed to rebalance back to equal weighting in the (now) £9500 invested in tracking the index	Weighting by value in index at start of the following quarter
Northumbrian Water	250	25%	1000	-10%	23.7%	55 purchased	25%
Pennon	500	25%	500	+20%	31.6%	105 sold	25%
Severn Trent	1000	25%	250	-10%	23.7%	14 purchased	25%
United Utilities	500	25%	500	-20%	21%	95 purchased	25%

The example just shows the rebalancing of equally weighted indices. Left to its own devices, any index tends towards cap-weighting as soon as it begins to track trading in the stock of its constituents. As far as an investor in an ETF tracking such an index is concerned, the quarterly rebalancing ensures that, while the index will not be perfectly equally weighted at all times, it does not move further and further away from being equally weighted.

5. Price-weighted indices

No survey of indices and weightings would be complete without a mention of the weighting scheme of the world's very first stock indices, the Dow Jones Transportation Average (started in 1884) and the much more famous Dow Jones Industrial Average, the Dow (started in 1896). Both of these began as price-weighted indices for the simple reason that price-weighting was the only kind that was practicable at the time.[53]

---

[53] The oldest UK index, the FT 30, originally known as the Financial News Ordinary and dating from 1935, is a price-weighted index but one that uses geometric averages. The Nikkei 225 index is another that is based on an arithmetic average of prices.

A price-weighted index is one where the weighting of a particular stock in the index is decided by its price – a stock with a higher price per share will have a greater effect on the overall index. For instance, if an index is comprised of two stocks trading at $75 (Company A) and $25 (Company B) respectively, the index will be weighted 75% towards Company A and 25% towards Company B.

Although the Dow is limited to just 30 stocks and still uses price-weighting, it generally stays fairly close to the S&P 500. A number of ETFs track the Dow Jones Industrial Average, including the State Street Global Advisors' Diamonds[54] Trust, which dates from 1998.

Free float adjustment and stock capping

Two further factors that may affect the performance of an ETF tracking an index are **free float adjusting** and **stock capping**. We will look at these in turn here.

Free float adjusting

Free float adjusting is a refinement to index theory introduced by Frank Russell Associates in 1984.[55] The insight behind it is that a company could have a big enough market capitalisation to qualify for inclusion in an index and yet at the same time shares in the company could be so illiquid that high trading volumes could cause wild fluctuations in the share price. When thinking about ETFs, indices that have a robust policy on free float adjusting are more suitable for tracking than those that do not. An ETF tracking an index that is not free float adjusted may well run into problems arising from replicating illiquid shares that have large weightings.[56]

---

[54] D(Dow) I(Industrial) A(Average) – monds; unfortunately ETF sponsors seem to have given up on thinking up such investor-friendly fund names.

[55] Russell indexes claim that free float adjusting has been an industry standard for a number of years but the approach of different index publishers varies considerably.

[56] The 'Further reading' section of this chapter looks at recent problems encountered by the DAX with free float adjusting and stock capping.

The FTSE and free float adjusting[57]

There are two elements to free float adjusting.

The first is to calculate the proportion of a company's market capitalisation that is highly unlikely to be traded. For instance, a company with a very large minority shareholder would have its free float adjusted downwards. In the case of the FTSE 100 (and other FTSE indices) a free float of less than 15% – meaning that 85% of the shares are held by a very few shareholders, who are unlikely to be interested in selling them – would disqualify the company from being a constituent. However, if a company has a free float of above that proportion the whole of its capitalisation is taken into account when the quarterly review is undertaken.

The second consideration is the cap-weighting to allow to a company that has large restricted shareholdings. The FTSE's approach to this is to have free float bands so that a company with a free float of 45%, for example, is in the 40-50% band and qualifies for 50% of its market capitalisation to be taken into consideration when deciding its index weighting. This means that with a FTSE 100 ETF, the exposure of the ETF to the free float adjusted company is correspondingly reduced. Some indices allow surprisingly small free floats; the DAX, Deutsche Boerse's large cap index, allowed free floats of as little as 5% until late last year.

Free float adjusting usually passes without comment in the media. For example, when the UK government acquired shares in Royal Bank of Scotland and Lloyds plc late in 2008, these banks' cap-weighting was simultaneously adjusted up, to allow for the new shares, and downwards, to take into account the reduction in their free float.

---

[57] Other restrictions on the free float of a share include cross-holdings between companies (so called 'trade investments'), founding families shareholdings, employee share schemes, government stakes and restrictions on foreign ownership.

Stock capping

Stock capping places a ceiling on the proportion of an index that can be made up of a particular stock or group of stocks. This has the effect of making an index more diverse (by allowing smaller stocks to be included in the index) and reducing exposure to a single large stock. For example, in May 2005 the market capitalisation of China Mobile should have given it a cap-weighting of 23% in the FTSE Xinhua 25 index (FXI 25). A fund tracking that index with a single constituent accounting for almost a quarter of its value would be too much akin to a strategy of tracking the other 24 companies in the index but lumped together with a China Mobile share stake. In fact the rules of the FXI 25 cap the China Mobile weighting at just over 11%.[58]

Funds tracking indices with very large individual constituents may fall foul of regulators' rules about diversification within collective investment vehicles (for more on this see Chapter 4). Stock capping overcomes this problem, albeit in a way that some may consider calls into question the fund's credentials as a truly passive investment.

Summary

The key points when thinking about ETFs and indices are:

- It is important to understand the index an ETF tracks. Most important is how the index constituents qualify for inclusion in the index and then how they are weighted once included.

- Indices were formerly all about cap-weighting; there are alternatives (such as fundamental-weighting) but it is debatable whether these count as passive investing. If the attraction of ETFs is that they are not managed – i.e. they are passive index trackers – then it should be borne in mind that some index construction methods may undermine this.

- Index construction is often blamed for making an ETF investment overweight or underweight in certain companies or sectors.

---

[58] Paul Hoff, FTSE Tradable Indices Presentation, June 2005. iShares have had an ETF tracking this index since October 2004 (the FTSE/Xinhua China 25 Index Fund).

- Tracking a particular country index will not necessarily capture investment returns that match the country's economic growth. A country index tracker will miss out on the success of nationalised industries, family or foreign controlled conglomerates, and small businesses. Also, some so-called national equity indices, such as the FTSE 100 or France's CAC 40, may be very international in terms of where their constituents make money or employ staff.

- On the whole, up until now, indices and index tracking have been increasing in refinement and complexity. The corollary of this is that the oldest ETFs track the most well-known indices.

- There has been a long-term outperformance of growth-style investments by value-style ones.

- The index construction method may affect the running expenses of the ETF. If the ETF is more expensive to run this will affect the returns of those investing in it.

Chapters 3 and 4 will look at the range of investments that index-tracking ETFs offer.

Further reading

Ways of looking at cap-weighting

Generally, the case against cap-weighted indices boils down to the argument that share prices are opinions (on the part of investors) masquerading as facts. Supporters of cap-weighting would argue although share prices may not measure companies' values perfectly, they are all that is to hand and, more specifically, inaccurate though they may be, there is no way of knowing for certain in which direction they are inaccurate.

Professor Jeremy Siegel, who has worked in cooperation with WisdomTree, set out the case against cap-weighting in an article entitled 'The **Noisy Market Hypothesis**' in June 2006. Since then this title has become a shorthand summation of the views held by advocates of fundamental-weighting.

Volkswagen: a cautionary tale about free floats and stock capping

The main interest of this case study is what happened to the stock indices (primarily the DAX 30 and the DJ Stoxx 600 Automobiles and Parts sector index) and funds that track them, but a little background detail is necessary first.

A spike in the price of Volkswagen shares in late October 2008 was caused by extensive short trading in VW shares when, unbeknown to the short traders, Porsche had control (through options) of 74% of the shares. With the German state of Lower Saxony controlling 20% and index-tracking funds about a further 6%, there were simply no investable shares left for short traders to close out their positions with. As a result the price of VW shares rose from €200 to €900 in just four days.

The immediate losers were the hedge funds that had been shorting VW shares but the episode raised important questions for ETF investors as well. At one stage VW shares accounted for 64% of the DJ Stoxx 600 Automobile sector index and 27% of the DAX 30. Investors' so-called passive investments were in fact giving them very high exposure to a single stock.

The DAX 30 did have a 10% stock cap in place but this was only applied on a quarterly basis. In the event the index publisher, Deutsche Boerse, applied the cap to VW as an immediate emergency measure. For its part DJ Stoxx announced that the free float adjustment for VW shares would be reduced by about a quarter.

The lesson from this in terms of ETFs is that free float adjusting and stock capping can be important. The FTSE 100 does have a capped version in which the weighting of individual stocks is capped at 5% (as at 31 December 2008 BP, HSBC, Vodafone, GlaxoSmithKline and Royal Dutch Shell A shares all had weightings of more than 5% on the uncapped FTSE 100) but most ETFs tracking the FTSE 100 are still tracking the uncapped version.

The wider issue of the general liquidity of ETFs is examined in Chapter 8.

Chapter 3

How an ETF Works

The sponsor of an ETF might describe the purpose of the fund in the following way:

> *The ETF's shares are ownership interests in the fund; they are intended to provide results that generally correspond to the price and yield of the index being tracked.*
>
> or
>
> *The investment objective of the ETF is to track the performance of the index.*

The basic purpose of ETFs, then, is to track their benchmark indices as closely as possible, to operate with a low cost and to be tradable throughout each trading day.

This chapter looks at the major ETF construction methods. These are explained at this stage with reference to equity ETFs only as these remain the most important category of ETF. However, the implications of using the different methods of construction are broadly similar for ETFs tracking other asset classes and for exchange traded commodities (ETCs).[59]

Why the mechanics of ETFs are important

ETF sponsors' marketing materials tend not to dwell on how ETFs work, partly because these intricacies detract from the theme that ETFs simplify investing. However, there may be times when the way in which an ETF is constructed could have a significant impact on its performance and this is why we take some time to examine the different methods of ETF construction in Chapter 3.

---

[59] Factors that are specific to the creation of other kinds of ETF and exchange traded commodities are dealt with in Chapters 4 and 5.

All ETFs broadly achieve the objective of tracking the performance of their underlying index, or other asset, but they do not all use the same method to do this. The three main approaches used to achieve index tracking are:

1. full **in-kind replication**

2. swap-based

3. **partial in-kind replication**

The method used for the first ETFs was full in-kind replication and this remains the most common design in the US. In this chapter we will look at full in-kind replication first of all before going on to examine the other main method of construction, the swap-based ETF, which is the predominant method of ETF creation in Europe. In the UK, most ETFs are either swap-based or use partial in-kind replication.

The examples used in this chapter are all of equity ETFs but the principles of ETF construction apply to ETFs for most other asset types too, such as fixed-income ETFs.

ETFs – the key roles

Before we look at the different methods of ETF construction, it is important to define some of the key roles involved in these processes. The main players involved with the creation of ETFs are listed in Table 3.1.

Table 3.1 – The key ETF roles

Role	Definition
Sponsor[60]	The company that creates, markets and administers the ETF, sometimes known as the ETF issuer, manager or provider. The sponsor is not responsible for creating ETF shares; this function requires the contribution of authorised participants (see below).
Exchange	By definition all ETFs are exchange tradable so they have to meet the listing requirements of the exchange they are traded on. In Europe it is common for ETFs to have multiple listings.
Market-makers	Firms that have engaged with the ETF's sponsor and the exchange to maintain a market in the shares of the ETF. In so doing they subject themselves to rules about trading spreads and minimum stake sizes that they will quote prices for. The presence of market-makers has the effect of guaranteeing market liquidity in an ETF's shares.
Index compiler	Index ETF sponsors will require a licence from the publisher of the index the product is based upon. Thus the Lyxor ETF FTSE 250 requires a licence from FTSE to use the FTSE 250 index.[61]
Market participants (MPs), (or authorised participants)	MPs create ETF shares for purchase. They are sometimes referred to as **creation unit holders**, primary traders or market participants. The process by which these ETF shares are created is described below. The relationship between the ETF sponsor and the ETF's market participant is analogous to that between a fast food franchisor and a franchisee. The franchisor (sponsor) has complete control over the product concept but it is the franchisee (market participant) that bakes the pizzas. Market participants will often be in the ETF's shares as well. The role of the market participant is the pivotal one in the operation of ETFs.

---

[60] Even at this stage ambiguity in terms muddies the waters. The Deutsche Boerse (in other words the Frankfurt stock exchange) and some other markets use **designated sponsor** to mean a market maker. For this reason, a German ETF sponsor such as Deutsche Bank will tend to avoid referring to themselves as such, preferring the label 'ETF fund manager'. To confuse matters even more, an ETF sponsor can also be the designated sponsor (i.e. market-maker) for its own ETF. Thus Société Générale's trading arm is normally one of the market-makers for each of the ETFs that have Lyxor as fund sponsor.

[61] The ETF does not need to trade on the home exchange of the index it tracks. Thus the iShares S&P 500 tracks the same American index as the SPDR Index 500 but is traded on the London Stock Exchange – it is an ETF for European investors to buy if they want to track the S&P 500. As we shall see, tracking foreign indices is one of the key advantages of ETFs.

Full in-kind replication

The full in-kind replication model consists of an ETF sponsor, on deciding to start an ETF, approaching an authorised participant. The authorised participant supplies the sponsor with a basket of thousands of shares in companies in the index the ETF will be tracking. This basket replicates the make-up of the index and is called a **creation unit**.[62]

The ETF sponsor then breaks the contents of the creation unit down into shares in the ETF, which can be traded on the stock exchange, and issues these ETF shares to the authorised participant. At the time of their creation the ETF's shares will be tiny replicas of the creation unit, which itself exactly replicated the index at the time the in-kind transfer was made. Typically, there are 25,000 or 50,000 ETF shares to each creation unit but the multiple can be smaller or larger than these amounts.

This whole process is an in-kind transfer since stocks are presented by the authorised participant to the ETF sponsor, rather than cash, in exchange for shares in the ETF. Since the creation basket and ETF shares fully replicate the index being tracked this construction method is known as full, **in-kind replication**.[63]

The shares in the ETF are what investors will buy and sell. These are not bought directly from the ETF sponsor, but from the authorised participant. As we saw in Chapter 1, ETFs, like investment funds, have the ability to create and cancel their shares all the time and this happens in response to fluctuations in investor demand. When someone wishes to buy shares in an ETF this is transmitted to the market-maker, and this then triggers an increase or decrease in the total number of ETF shares in existence.

---

[62] This transaction is in fact a three-way one: firstly between the authorised participant and the institution acting as the custodian for the exchange traded fund, which receives the basket of shares; secondly between the custodian and the sponsor of the ETF, which is notified that the basket of shares (creation unit) has been received; and lastly by the issue of ETF shares by the custodian on behalf of the ETF. The important point is that the contents of these creation baskets are in the safekeeping of a custodian bank; these underlying assets can't be embezzled.

[63] Sometimes labels such as 'physical' or 'in-specie' are used to describe this model of ETF creation. Describing them as **cash-based** seems even more confusing, as keeping the transaction in-kind is how the close tracking effect is achieved.

This section will explore how shares in an ETF are created and how the process which enables the shares to be traded works.

> ## Example of the replication method
>
> The replication method can be best illustrated with a hypothetical example of a water utilities ETF, based upon the cap-weighted version of our notional index of large water utilities with stock exchange listings. Our notional index is comprised of these four companies in the following proportions:
>
> - Northumbrian Water (15%)
> - Pennon (20%)
> - Severn Trent (27%)
> - United Utilities (38%)
>
> The aggregate value of the shares of each company that would go into the creation basket for this ETF would match these proportions. Thus the creation basket replicates our notional index exactly. Furthermore, each share of the ETF has the same make-up as the creation basket and the index, so that 38% of each ETF share's underlying assets is equity in United Utilities, 27% is equity in Severn Trent, and so on.

The classic in-kind transaction is shown in Figure 3.1.

Figure 3.1 – Classic in-kind ETF share creation[64]

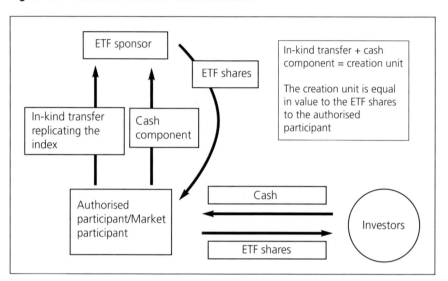

The cash component paid by the authorised participant covers any part of the transfer that cannot be paid in kind. For example, there might be dividends that have been paid by index constituents to the ETF but which have not been paid out to the ETF's shareholders.[65] Sometimes, the cash component may be required to cover the purchase of shares on the index because the shares of one of the companies in the index have been suspended from trading.

---

[64] This diagram assumes that the authorised participant/market participant is also a market-maker for the ETF in question on the secondary market. The role and number of market-makers for an ETF depends on the fund sponsor and on the exchange on which the ETF is listed. Not all authorised participants will be carrying out a market-making role in order to enable ordinary investors to buy or sell the ETF's shares. Some may be in the role solely to exploit **arbitrage** opportunities. The authorised participant may borrow the stocks for the in-kind transfer rather than own them.

[65] More information about the place of dividends in ETFs is included in the section 'swap-based ETFs are a European arrangement' on page 58 and in the 'Further reading' section of this chapter on page 60.

The ETF redemption process and ETF pricing

To see the full significance of the ETF creation process it needs to be looked at in conjunction with ETF redemptions. Although the ETF share price is subject to the level of demand for the shares on the secondary market, it is the cycle of creation and redemption of ETF shares by authorised participants that maintains the alignment between the ETF share price and the index that it is tracking. For an ETF, the price of each share should be very close to the net asset value of the ETF. The process for ETF redemptions is shown in Figure 3.2.

Figure 3.2 – Classic in-kind ETF share redemption

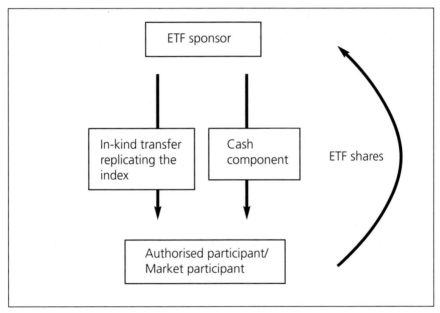

The incentive for authorised participants to engage in the creation and redemption of ETF shares is the **arbitrage** opportunity presented to them in fulfilling this role. The best way to understand this is to take a hypothetical example.

Example: an arbitrage opportunity for an authorised participant

In this example the ETF is trading at a discount to its NAV. For whatever reason, the price of the ETF shares is lagging behind the index that it is supposed to track.

Price of ETF shares: 150.0

ETF share NAV: 151.5

In these circumstances the authorised participant has an arbitrage opportunity through transferring one redemption unit – this being 50,000 ETF shares in the case of this particular fund – back to the ETF sponsor. The exchange traded fund will redeem the ETF shares by returning the basket of constituents' shares (and cash component) that a creation unit is comprised of to the authorised participant.

In this example, the value of the 50,000 ETF shares that have been redeemed is £75,000 (£1.50 x 50,000) but the value of the basket of stocks returned to the authorised participant will be £75,750 (£1.515 x 50,000).[66]

The authorised participant now has shares (in companies on the index) worth £750 more than the ETF shares that it transferred back to the exchange traded fund. The authorised participant will then sell the shares. The net result is that the number of the ETF's shares in issue will have been reduced.

The action of reducing the supply of ETFs will cause a small upward pressure on the ETF price. And the action of selling the index component company shares back into the market will have a small downward pressure on the prices of those shares. The result is that the price of the ETF will move towards its NAV. The repeated arbitrage action of the authorised participants will cause the gap between ETF and its NAV to close.

Were the ETF shares at a premium to their NAV and the index they track, the authorised participant's arbitrage opportunity would be to put together more creation units from the (relatively cheap) shares in the index in order to create extra (relatively expensive) ETF shares.

---

[66] This example demonstrates the effect of the creation/redemption processes but in real life the processes have an extra level of sophistication; this is examined in the 'Further reading' section of this chapter.

The repetition of the creation and redemption processes is the mechanism that enables the ETF to track its index. As far as the authorised participant is concerned, although the profit on one particular creation or redemption may be small, the arbitrage profit is free of risk. From the point of view of the market the continual cycle of arbitrage opportunities and re-adjustments of ETF price to NAV represents a huge advance on the premium/discount problem of the traditional investment trust.

How to track an ETF's NAV through the trading day

An ETF's premium or discount to its index's NAV can be followed by looking at the **intraday value** of the ETF, often referred to as the **intraday indicative value** or IIV.

The IIV is an estimation of net asset value of the index being tracked and is normally presented at 15 second intervals throughout the trading day. This indicator is obviously of enormous importance for arbitrageurs in deciding whether to create or redeem units in the ETF.

Normally, an ETF's intraday indicative value will have its own symbol. In the US IIVs have the same ticker symbol as the fund itself but with the extension IV instead of the normal extension denoting the exchange. Deutsche Boerse gives indices tracked by funds listed on the exchange an iNAV. Publication of iNAV data minute by minute is a requirement of Deutsche Boerse, Euronext and Borsa Italia but, at the time of writing, the London Stock Exchange does not have a similar requirement or make such a service available. The websites of ETF sponsors will often provide the IIV but this may depend upon which exchange the ETF is traded on.

One drawback with intraday values is that they can only update if the exchange of the index being tracked is open for trading. It is important to also be aware that iNAV may be expressed in the **trading currency** of the ETF instead of the **index currency**.[67]

---

[67] The differences between index currencies and trading currencies is dealt with in detail in Chapter 8, in 'ETFs and currencies'.

The popularity of ETFs in the US – a note on the ETF redemption process

The tax efficiency of ETFs in the United States has given a huge boost to their popularity because ETFs are taxed differently to US mutual funds.

US mutual funds have to distribute realised capital gains to their investors, who may have to pay tax on them. This is different to European investment funds, because in Europe investors only realise a capital gain when they decide to sell their own investment in the fund.

ETFs in America get around this flaw in the mutual fund model by using (index constituent) shares with the lowest **cost basis** when authorised participants come to redeem the ETF's shares. In the redemption process the authorised participant gets back all the constituent companies' shares in the right proportions but the sponsor endeavours to use those shares of each constituent that were acquired by the fund most cheaply. Thus a steady flow of redemptions has the effect of constantly flushing out the holdings with the lowest cost basis and increasing the cost basis of the fund as a whole.

The United States has been the world's leader in ETFs and many ground-breaking developments originate there. Whenever reading US commentators on the ETF industry, it is worth remembering that the capital gains advantages of ETFs (based on the in-kind replication that US ETFs use) compared to mutual funds may colour their approach.

Swap-based ETF share creation

The swap-based ETF, sometimes known as the **synthetic replication** ETF, is the second most common construction method and this is the design that predominates in Europe. Before explaining the swap-based method of replicating index performance it is necessary to introduce a further category of player in the ETF industry, one which is vital to the design of this type of ETF – the *swap counterparty*.

A swap counterparty guarantees the return for the ETF. It is normally a bank, very often the parent bank of the ETF sponsor.[68] This guarantee by the counterparty enables the ETF to match the return of the index it aims to replicate.

The purpose of a swap-based ETF's is the same as that of an ETF that conforms to the classic full replication model. Both are tradable instruments, both will track an index and both have creation and redemption processes. However, beneath the surface similarities, there is an important difference between the two models.

Although the swap-based model has creation and redemption processes, these do not enable the ETF to track its index, unlike the full replication model's cycle of share creations and redemptions. Creation in a swap-based ETF is merely the way in which it increases its size, in terms of numbers of ETF shares in issue. *The swap-based ETF's tracking ability derives from the swap counterparty's guarantee.*

The creation process begins with the market participant paying cash or equities to the ETF sponsor in exchange for shares in the ETF.[69] The sponsor has more flexibility in stipulating what is required from the market participant than is the case with an ETF created by full in-kind replication because the ETF's tracking does not depend upon it.

The swap agreement

For swap-based ETFs the tracking ability depends upon the swap agreement. This is an agreement with the swap counterparty, who guarantees to the ETF sponsor to provide a return that matches that of the underlying asset or index. In return for this guarantee the swap counterparty will receive the **substitute basket** from the ETF sponsor.[70] There is no need for the substitute basket to

---

[68] ETF sponsor ETF Securities introduced a new scheme for multiple swap counterparties in spring 2009 with its **ETF Exchange** platform, set up in cooperation with 15 financial institutions. Up until then all swap-based ETFs each had a single swap counterparty.

[69] Swap-based ETF managers/sponsors will normally restrict creation and redemption to large institutions, and may refer to them as authorised participants.

[70] The swap counterparty may charge a swap fee in addition.

replicate the index being tracked by the ETF although, if the ETF is tracking an equity index (as opposed, say, to a bond ETF), it would normally comprise stocks. In effect, control or use of the substitute basket is the payment that the swap counterparty receives for taking on the risk of guaranteeing that the ETF will replicate its index.[71] The swap-based process is illustrated in Figure 3.3.

Figure 3.3 – Swap-based ETF share creation and replication

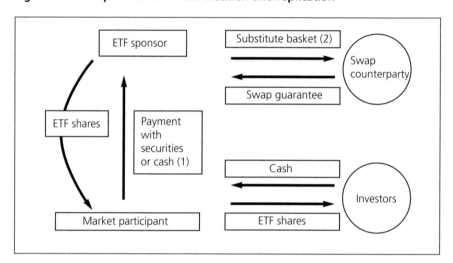

The payment (1) by the market participant may be similar or even identical to the contents of the substitute basket (2). The swap-based method of replication leaves the ETF sponsor with a measure of flexibility on this.

The swap-based method of ETF construction gives rise to a number of important considerations:

Avoidance of tracking differences

Tracking differences can be avoided completely with swap-based ETFs. Tracking the world's foremost stock exchange indices may not present a serious problem for full replication ETFs, but for in-kind ETFs that track more

---

[71] The contents of the substitute basket remains confidential information between the ETF sponsor and the swap counterparty.

obscure indices there may be difficulties with, for example, putting together a creation basket. When full replication becomes difficult, index tracking is placed in jeopardy. Swap-based ETFs get around these problems and as such can be used to track a wider variety of asset types.

Counterparty risk

The successful tracking of the index depends upon the guarantee given by the swap counterparty. This means that there is a counterparty risk – the counterparty may default on its swap agreements. A default by a counterparty such as an investment bank could be triggered by losses in its swaps business but equally it could be as a result of bad loans, rogue traders or investments in sub-prime mortgages; the damage to the ETF would be the same in any case. Although the substitute basket of shares will act as collateral, the price of the substitute basket and the index being tracked are bound to diverge so some risk will remain.[72]

Regulatory requirements on diversification

Swap-based ETFs may enable the sponsor to get around regulatory requirements regarding diversification. For example, UCITS III stipulates that UCITS' compliant funds should not be invested in any single constituent investment above 20% of the fund's NAV.[73] This 20% ceiling is easily reached by ETFs tracking some sector indices. For instance, the DJ STOXX 600 Technology index's two largest component stocks, Nokia and SAP, comprise 31.5% and 20.7% of the index respectively. A swap-based ETF tracking that index overcomes this regulatory restriction because the fund has invested in the swap rather than the actual index constituents. It is important to note that the investor does not avoid the high level of exposure to the big index constituent. However, an ETF prospectus will refer to this exposure as an investment risk as opposed to a counterparty risk.

---

[72] The way in which UCITS III regulates counterparty risk in swap-based ETFs is covered in the 'Further reading' section of this chapter.

[73] National regulators have the discretionary power to permit a fund to increase this cap to 35%.

Payment of dividends

Swap-based ETFs simplify the payment of dividends. Whereas a full replication ETF has real dividends from the index constituents to distribute with time lags and, possibly, dividend (and withholding) taxes to contend with, the swap-based ETF simply covers dividends within the swap counterparty agreement. Among other things, this gives them a great advantage if the index being tracked is a **total return index** (with dividends being rolled up the index).[74]

Swap-based ETFs are a European arrangement

Swap-based ETFs are mainly a European phenomenon and in the US they are not currently permitted.[75] Within the European Union most ETFs are swap-based but some work according to the full replication model. The leading providers of swap-based ETFs are db x-trackers and Lyxor. The largest European ETF sponsor in terms of assets under management – iShares – is also the leading proponent of the in-kind replication model.[76] However, the iShares DJ STOXX 600 range of sector ETFs are swap-based.[77] A provider with a mixture of fully replicated and swap-based ETFs is easyETF, which is a joint venture between AXA and BNP Paribas (Banque Nationale de Paris).

---

[74] This is not to say that swap-based ETFs never pay dividends. If the ETF is tracking an ordinary stock exchange index, it probably will. However, as the fund is not invested in the index but just replicating it, the dividends will be created synthetically also. The tax treatment of dividends in countries such as Germany is a key reason for the preference for swap-based ETFs.

[75] The only current exceptions to this principle are leveraged and short ETFs where the US Securities & Exchange Commission (SEC) has permitted swaps and options and derivatives, generally for creating ETF shares (Release No. 34-56684; 22 October 2007).

[76] In fact the majority of iShares' ETFs work on the **optimised replication** model rather than full replication (see the next section 'Other models of ETF construction'). Their policy of favouring in-kind replication presumably owes much to iShares' major presence in the US as an ETF provider.

[77] iShares has 18 swap-based ETFs, all domiciled in Germany and all tracking sector indices. The swap counterparty is HypoVereinsbank, part of UnoCredito. In October 2010 iShares announced the launch of ETFs tracking Indian and Russian indices that would be listed on the London Stock Exchange; these would both have multiple swap counterparties.

Other models of ETF construction

While full replication and swap-based ETFs are the most important types, there are a few other kinds.

Representative sampling strategy

Probably the most common of these variants is known as partial in-kind replication or **representative sampling strategy**. This is a variation of the full replication model where the ETF holds stocks that reflect the performance of the index the ETF is tracking, but does not hold the full index. This makes it easier for market participants to put together a creation basket in circumstances where one or more of the stocks in the index is illiquid or the sheer size of the index makes full replication awkward. The disadvantage of representative sampling strategy is that the ETF will not track the index as closely as an ETF that fully replicates the index (or a swap-based ETF).

Clearly, the sponsor of an ETF based on representative sampling will have to publish a list of the stocks required for an acceptable creation basket and what an authorised participant can expect to receive back in a redemption basket.

Representative sampling strategies are permitted in the US and seem to be the preferred model for Swiss-domiciled ETFs. The model may also be referred to as **optimisation** or **optimised replication.**

Use of futures contracts to replicate the performance of an index

Another method of replication is the use of futures contracts by the sponsor to replicate the performance of an index. This method of replication comes under the heading 'synthetic', together with swap-based replication. The Société Générale Asset Management (SGAM) Index US ETF is an example of an ETF that uses futures to replicate the performance of its index.

A combination approach to tracking

Some ETF sponsors may combine two share creation models into a hybrid. It's quite common for an ETF's investment objectives to anticipate possible difficulties with full replication by allowing for a combination of full replication and swap, or permitting authorised participants to make up some or all of the creation basket with cash instead of stocks.

The merits of the different methods of ETF construction

There has been some debate amongst commentators about the relative merits of the full replication model and the swap-based model for ETFs. In particular, the onset of the credit crunch in 2008 brought the subject of counterparty risk under increased scrutiny. One solution to the problem is for each ETF to operate with multiple swap counterparties, thus reducing the impact of any one of them defaulting on their swap obligation. This is the approach adopted by the sponsors Source and ETF Securities. The phrase *third generation ETF* was coined to describe this method of ETF creation.

On the plus side, swap-based ETFs and ETFs based on optimisation undoubtedly offer greater versatility, allowing ETFs to enter new territory where poor market liquidity might make it difficult to put together creation baskets for fully replicated funds.

Further reading

Detailed example of the ETF share creation and redemption processes

As mentioned in footnote 66 the example of ETF creation and redemption given earlier was simplified in order to emphasise the vital effect of arbitrage. This more detailed description uses the same example as the section 'Example: an arbitrage opportunity for an authorised participant' on page 52 but restores some important details that are present in these transactions in real life.

In the earlier example the ETF was trading at a discount of 1.5 pence to its NAV, and the authorised participant would undertake the following transactions:

Simultaneously:

- buy sufficient ETF shares to make up a creation unit – £75,000
- short sell the index (i.e. the stocks that comprise the index)[78] – £75,750
- place a redemption order for one creation unit of the ETF.

Next:

- deliver the ETF shares to settle for the basket of stocks that equal a creation unit
- receive back the basket of stocks.

If the ETF was trading at a premium to its NAV, the process would be reversed as follows:

Simultaneously:

- short sell the ETF shares (equal in number to the size of a creation unit).
- buy the index (i.e. buy enough stocks in the right proportions for a creation unit)
- place a creation order for one creation unit.

Next:

- deliver the creation basket
- receive in exchange 50,000 ETF shares.

The combination of actions concurrently guarantees the arbitrage advantage to the authorised participant. If these stages are followed consecutively, that is if they were to wait to receive the basket of index shares through settlement of the ETF share redemption and then sell the index, they would open themselves to the risk of prices moving in the meantime.

---

[78] The authorised participant would probably borrow the stocks required to short sell the index here. In this case the returned basket of stocks (E) would be used to close out the short.

UCITS III, ETFs and swap counterparty risk

Under UCITS III a fund is not permitted to risk more than 10% of its NAV[79] in derivatives, including **equity linked swaps** in general and index swaps. This is *not* a ceiling on the proportion of the ETF that is swap-based – an ETF can be 100% swap-based – but a cap on the amount of counterparty risk the swap exposes the ETF to. The ETF must not expose its shareholders to a counterparty risk (a risk that the counterparty will not be able to honour its obligations under the swap) that amounts to more than 10% of its NAV.

The substitute basket used in the ETF share creation continues in existence, acting as collateral for the swap agreement the ETF has made with the swap counterparty. Risk arises when the substitute basket collateral ceases to match the index in terms of price.

In practice the ETF and its swap counterparty abide by the UCITS III regulation in the following way:

How the ETF sponsor and swap counterparty abide by UCITS' regulation

At the time of share creation the substitute basket and the index swap should have equal value.

If the index rises more than the substitute basket the ETF's exposure to the swap is calculated as ETF NAV, less the value of the substitute basket, divided by 100.

$$\frac{(ETF\ NAV\ -\ substitute\ basket)}{100} = ETF\ exposure\ to\ swap$$

---

[79] If the swap provider is a bank from outside the European Union or a non-bank the UCITS' requirement is a counterparty risk of no more than 5%.

If the index exposure to the swap approaches 10% the swap will need to be reset. The swap counterparty will pay the ETF the difference between the index and the substitute basket and this payment will be used to invest in more shares to be incorporated into the substitute basket. The effect of this resetting is to reduce the counterparty exposure back to zero.

In the event that the market moves in the opposite direction so that the index is at a discount to the substitute basket, stocks from the substitute basket will be sold off with the proceeds going to the swap counterparty. The counterparty exposure moves from almost 10% to zero.

Some ETF providers take a much more conservative approach to potential counterparty risks than UCITS III's minimum standard. For example, db x-trackers has a policy of adjusting the collateral (in the substitute basket) on a daily basis instead of waiting for the swap exposure to reach a particular level before an adjustment is made.

Lyxor ETF takes a somewhat different approach in that the swap is generally limited to 10% of the fund's assets but the fund obtains index tracking for the whole of itself from the swap counterparty.[80]

The effect of dividends on an ETF's performance

Just as the price of a company's shares may increase in the lead up to the ex-dividend date and then fall back once the share has gone ex-dividend, ETF share prices can also be distorted by dividends. The reason for this effect is that, for reasons of simple administrative efficiency, ETFs do not normally

---

[80] Securities Note Relating to the Lyxor ETF FTSE 250. At the time of writing, Société Générale, Lyxor's parent, was the sole swap counterparty. However, although Lyxor has stated that it is theoretically open to swaps with other counterparties, it looks as if these other counterparties would want some say on the contents of the substitute basket.

pay out dividends as soon as they are received from constituent companies. Instead a dividend-paying ETF will have its own quarterly or half yearly dividend dates like shares in an individual company. This means that as the quarter progresses the fund's value grows with all the dividends that have accrued from the fund's constituents during that quarter. This can mean that the ETF's NAV (and thus share price) diverges (upwards) somewhat from the index until the quarterly dividend payment date is passed.

While the distinction between ETFs tracking total return indices (where the dividends are treated as being re-invested) and ordinary equity indices (where the dividends are treated as being paid) is clear cut, sponsors' information about ETFs can sometimes be confusing on this score. For example:

- iShares MSCI AC Far East ex-Japan ETF says it aims to give a total return "taking into account both capital and income returns" – in other words this ETF tracks an ordinary equity index and pays a dividend, but re-invests it on the behalf of the investor.

- EasyETF has dividend-paying and **accumulating** versions of ETFs that track the same index, the DJ EURO STOXX 50.

ETFs and rights issues

Following forecasts that Europe-wide stock market capital raising could reach €380 billion in the near future,[81] it is appropriate to look at how ETFs handle rights issues.

ETF's prospectuses provide no mechanism for an ETF to take up or sell on rights. The index-tracking ETF will always follow the passive route of doing just that. This is somewhat different from a holder of shares in individual companies behaving in a passive manner. Those investors would allow their rights to lapse but would probably have them sold on by the investment bank organising the rights issue. The ETF is blind to any actions affecting individual constituents' shares – it only sees the behaviour of the whole index.

---

[81] *Sunday Times*, 21 June 2009, quoting Peter Oppenheimer of Goldman Sachs.

If the ETF is based on in-kind replication, the sponsor will probably be engaged in a **stock-lending** programme. The terms of the stock lending may require the stock borrower to return the holding to the lender so that they can exercise their rights or may stipulate that when the loan of the stock is over, the shares plus the rights issue shares are returned to the lender.

However the ETF sponsor handles a rights issue situation, there may be profits arising from the issue that should be used to offset the costs of the ETF (and hence reduce its **total expense ratio**). It should be possible to set out, for the benefit of the ETF shareholders, just how much profit the sponsor makes from these incidental benefits arising from the ETF's shareholdings.

In the case of a swap-based ETF, the sponsor does not directly hold any of the shares in the index the ETF is tracking.

Whether the ETF achieves replication of the index by the in-kind method or the swap method, the rights issues will normally increase the market capitalisation of the company in question so an ETF tracking a cap-weighted index will end up increasing its holding in that company. By contrast, an ETF tracking a dividend weighted index probably will not register any change in its composition arising from a rights issue and one tracking an equally weighted index certainly will not change.

At the end of the process, an index-tracking ETF has missed out on the potential gains of taking up or selling on rights and avoided the potential losses that these actions might have incurred.

PART TWO:
The ETF Universe

Chapter 4

**Beyond Equities:
ETFs for Other Asset Classes**

Having looked at ETFs for equities in our examination of equity indices (Chapter 2) and how ETFs are constructed (Chapter 3), we now turn our attention to ETFs that track other asset classes. The asset classes we will look at are:

1. fixed-income securities

2. cash

3. currencies

4. credit

5. property.

Commodities investing through exchange traded instruments will be treated separately in Chapter 5 because commodity indices work in an entirely different manner from other indices.

1. Fixed-income ETFs

Fixed-income ETFs (otherwise known as fixed interest or bond ETFs) are designed to operate in the same way as equity ETFs – they track the performance of bond market indices. Bond market indices are compiled to represent the performance of the overall bond market, or of a specific sector of the bond market – for instance – government bonds, treasury bills or municipal bonds. Bond ETFs aim to match the performance of one or a number of these indices. As with equity ETFs there are two basic methods of fund construction: full, in-kind replication and swap-based.

There is a wide variety of underlying securities in the area of fixed-income ETFs and the bond indices used to measure performance can be obscure. Although ETFs may make fixed interest investing more straightforward, they do not make these investments any simpler or less risky overall; the complexity of the underlying asset remains.

At present the range of European-domiciled fixed interest ETFs does not match the full range of the asset class of fixed-income securities – ETFs domiciled in the United States cover a wider selection of the fixed interest spectrum. However, with fixed interest assets tripling in 2008, European-domiciled ETFs are catching up with the US. The growth of the market for fixed interest ETFs in Europe – from 16% to 27% by assets in 2008[82] – is partly a reflection of the importance of this type of asset to the continental European finance and savings industry.[83]

Table 4.1 – Fixed interest ETF coverage: the availability of products within US and European jurisdictions

Type of security	ETF coverage in the US	ETF coverage in Europe
Government bonds	Y	Y
(Price/cost of living) Index linked govt. bonds[84]	Y	Y
Treasury bills[85]	Y	
Municipal bonds	Y	86
Quasi-government bonds[87]	Y	
Investment grade bonds	Y	Y
High yield bonds (junk bonds)	Y	
Mortgage-backed securities (MBS)	Y[88]	89
Asset-backed securities (ABS)	90	
CMBS (Commercial MBS)	Y	
Hybrid ARMs (adjustable rate mortgages)[91]		
Aggregate bond index[92]	Y	

---

[82] Paul Amery, 'Bond Index ETFs' Performance Diverges in 2008', IndexUniverse, 30 December 2008.

[83] Fixed income makes up roughly half of the assets of Europe's mutual fund industry. (Marco Montanari, Head of Fixed-income ETFs, db x-trackers in London, quoted by IndexUniverse, 27 February 2009.) Despite the importance of fixed interest securities on the continental European financial scene, iShares was the only sponsor of European-domiciled fixed interest ETFs from 2003 to 2007.

[84] Known as TIPS (Treasury Inflation Protected Securities) in the United States.

[85] The definition of a US Treasury Bill is that maturity is no more than 12 months after issue.

[86] At the time of writing there are no European-domiciled ETFs tracking US municipal bonds or European ones. The only equivalent UK authority that has issued bonds recently is Transport for London.

[87] These are securities issued by quasi-government US institutions such as Fannie Mae and Freddie Mac. In Europe the European Investment Bank and the European Bank for Reconstruction & Development would probably qualify as quasi-government, and they do issue fixed interest securities, but none are tracked by ETFs.

[88] US MBS ETFs are a very new development. They should not be confused with MBS Bond ETFs where the bond is underwritten by a US federal agency (see footnote 87). ETFs for subprime debt have been discussed as one method of handling the so-called toxic assets in the US. Denmark is the only European country to have mortgage-backed securities but the credit-rating process and other controls on issuers are far stricter than has been the case in the US.

[89] An example of a European MBS-style security to be tracked by a European-domiciled ETF is the German Pfandbriefe. One vital consideration with Pfandbriefe is that they are not only backed by high grade mortgages but the issuers are fully liable for their repayment. The liability does *not* lie off-balance sheet in a special purpose vehicle as it might in the US. In reality, Pfandbriefe are closer to MBS bonds issued by the likes of Fannie Mae and Freddie Mac. Equivalents to Pfandbriefe exist in other European countries, such as the Spanish *cédula*; the generic name for them is 'covered bonds'. Although the dual backing of the issuer's creditworthiness and a mortgage may look impressive - these instruments can be affected by collapses in property prices and issuers' credit ratings happening at the same time.

[90] Asset-backed securities are included in the Barclays Aggregate Bond Index (see also footnote 92).

[91] US Hybrid ARMs are treated as a subset of MBS.

[92] The Barclays (formerly Lehman) Aggregate Bond Index now operated by Barclays Capital and tracked by iShares, Vanguard and SPDR ETFs. iShares also track the DEX Universe Bond Index (formerly Scotia Capital Universe Bond Index), which tracks Canadian fixed interest securities in a similar way. There are global and euro versions of the Aggregate Bond Index. iShares' Euro Aggregate Bond Fund began trading at the end of May 2009. The euro zone is also covered by the iBoxx Euro Overall index. It's worth noting that neither Indian nor Chinese government, nor corporate bonds, are constituents of any international bond indices.

Fixed-income indices

Bond indices tend to be weighted by market capitalisation based on clean prices (i.e. excluding interest accrued but not yet paid)[93] but may be equal-weighted. For government bonds, most index publishers will publish separate indices based on the lifespan of the bonds, for example, Barclays Euro Government Bond 5 Year Term Index. Index publishers may also have requirements about the time to run (also known as term to maturity) of the bonds that are included. There are some fixed-income indices that track bonds by their term to maturity instead of their lifespan. iShares iBoxx € Liquid Sovereigns Capped 5.5-10.5 (DE) is one example. There are indices of corporate bonds based on maturities as well.

The big difference between fixed-income indices and equity indices is that, unlike equities, there are no bond exchanges with fixed-income indices and therefore there is no central price reporting. In the past, fixed-income index compilers tended to be investment banks that initially relied upon their in-house bond trading operations to furnish them with the necessary data. More recently, and especially in Europe, fixed-income indices have tended to become more collaborative ventures.[94]

---

[93] A notable exception is PC Bond, the publisher of the DEX Universe and other Canadian bond indices, which uses dirty, or gross, prices (including interest accrued).

[94] The iBoxx index brand, the leading index compiler for euro and sterling bonds, is a consortium of European and US banks.

The spreads and liquidity of fixed-interest ETFs

Fixed-interest ETFs cover investments with an enormous range of liquidity. The liquidity of government bonds (as opposed to corporate bonds) is normally buoyed up by their attractiveness as a low risk alternative to cash. In the case of investment grade corporate bonds, there is often plenty of interest at the time of issue and very thin trading thereafter. High-yield bonds may be more liquid than investment grade ones because sentiment about the issuers is more volatile.

The novelty of passive, fixed-income investing

When tracing the development of equity investing, there is no question that index tracking has been gradually prevailing. It would seem perfectly natural to apply this approach to the fixed-income arena. However, it should be borne in mind that tracking fixed-income indices is a new development. At present there are no UK mutual funds that allow a fixed-income index to be tracked passively.

So, while fixed-income ETFs are undoubtedly one good method to consider when diversifying a portfolio, it should be remembered that they are not quite equivalent to other UK fixed-income investment funds (of which there are around 200).

There are additional considerations for those already familiar with investing in individual bonds who are thinking of moving into fixed-income ETFs. Firstly, a fixed-income ETF pays income like a share, not a bond. Unlike individual bonds where the outstanding coupon owing is incorporated into the dirty price of the security, investments in fixed-income ETFs will receive periodic dividend payments and so attention needs to be paid to ex-dividend dates.

Secondly, the assessment of a fixed-income ETF should not be exactly the same as for an individual bond. With individual bonds the yield to maturity (YTM) figure would normally be used as the basis for an evaluation of the bond in question; but with individual bonds the YTM will only change as a result of market factors such as changes in inflation or interest rate forecasts, or the choice of alternative bonds available. However, in the case of fixed-income ETFs the YTM may change as a result of the relevant index being rebalanced and the constituents of the ETF itself changing. Index rebalancing can occur as often as monthly.

One way to make investing in fixed-income ETFs clearer would be if information were supplied about the weighted coupon and par value of the ETF (i.e. the weighted averages of the ETF constituents for these two measures) alongside the price information, in a chart format. That way a better idea of the effect of index rebalancing on the ETF's performance could be obtained. This information could be made available by ETF sponsors, providers of price charts such as ADVN and price services such as Bloomberg and Reuters.

Convertible bond ETFs

There are a few US-domiciled ETFs that track convertible bond (bonds that convert to shares) indices such as the SPDR Barclays Capital Convertible Bond ETF. So far there are no European-domiciled ETFs in the convertibles section of the fixed-income market.

Preference share ETFs

As with convertibles, there are a number of US-domiciled ETFs that specialise in tracking preferred stock such as the Powershares Financial Preferred Portfolio[95] but, as yet, there are no European-domiciled equivalents.

---

[95] This ETF tracks the Wachovia Hybrid & Preferred Securities (WHPS) Financial Index.

When tracking breaks down[96]

In the market turmoil of autumn 2008, the market for US corporate bonds (both high grade and high yield) seized up almost entirely. The effect on fixed-income ETFs was striking. The iShares iBoxx Investment Grade Corporate Bond Fund reached a discount to its net asset value of 6% by 7 October. Discounts were much higher still on high yield bond ETFs such as the iShares iBoxx High Yield Corporate Bond Fund (28%) and Powershares High Yield ETF (15%). At the same time ETFs tracking municipal bond indices achieved substantial premiums to net asset value.

It appears that under these extreme conditions the ETF model for tracking indices broke down. These fixed-income ETFs with their large discounts or premiums were suddenly behaving more like old-style investment trusts.

The wide tracking differences may have been the fault of the ETFs but it might just as well have been the indices themselves that were at fault, showing false values because trading in their constituents was just too thin. It has even been suggested that, during this period, bond traders may have been taking their cue from fixed-income ETF prices instead of the other way around.

Even the ($9bn) iShares Capital Aggregate Bond Fund was affected by a substantial price drop (and discount to NAV) in October 2008, suggesting that many holders had no idea how such a broad index might perform in extreme conditions and decided that they would prefer to have cash. Normally this ETF trades in the relatively narrow range of $97 to $103 a share, but dropped to below $90 on 10 October. Since then the fund has recovered and behaved more like the low risk investment (for dollar investors) that it used to be.

---

[96] The idea that bond traders might have been using fixed-income ETFs for price discovery purposes did not create much of a stir at the time but it does raise some important questions about the way that the regulators treat tracking investments and the indices they are supposed to track. An ETF investor is indirectly paying the index compiler and it looks as if investors collectively are not getting a good deal if the index figures can't be relied on. Furthermore, it seems as if institutions could, theoretically, abuse the system, refusing to buy the underlying bonds but then investing in the fixed-income ETFs.

2. Cash ETFs

Among sponsors of European-domiciled ETFs, db x-trackers has the edge when it comes to cash (or money market) ETFs. Deutsche Bank is also the publisher of some of the most important money market indices. The main db x-tracker ETFs in this area are as follows:

- $ Money Market Cap ETF, which tracks the Federal Funds Total Return reflecting a daily rolled deposit earning the federal funds effective rate.

- EONIA (Euro Overnight Index Average) TR (Total Return) Index ETF, which tracks the money and capital markets of the euro zone.

- £ Money Market Cap ETF, which tracks the SONIA (Sterling Overnight Index Average) TR Index, representing the money and capital markets in the sterling area.

EasyETF is another sponsor with money market funds: EuroMTS Eonia, which tracks the EuroMTS Eonia Investable Index, and EuroMTS Fed Funds. EuroMTS Eonia Investable Index is also tracked by the Lyxor ETF Euro Cash. All three of these money market ETF sponsors use the swap-based approach.

Money market ETFs were particularly popular as a safe haven during the credit crunch in 2007-8, even though the real return after taking account of inflation was negative for part of that period. Assets under management for db x-trackers EONIA TR Index were €4.8bn in March 2009 while Lyxor ETF Euro Cash had €2.5bn of assets under management.[97]

It has been suggested that money market ETFs may find favour as a method of holding uninvested cash. However, in the case of the db x-trackers Sterling Money Market ETF there are some problems with using this approach. The fund, which has much lower assets under management than its euro counterpart, is subject to thin trading and relatively high spreads. This, coupled with dealing charges and the high price of the individual ETFs (approximately £180), could deter investors.

---

[97] For institutional investors money market ETFs are becoming an attractive alternative to certificates of deposit on account of their transparency and lower risk. (Paul Amery, 'Money Market ETFs in Europe', IndexUniverse, 21 July 2008.)

Money Market Indices

EONIA (Euro Overnight Index Average) – this is a weighted average of interest rates on unsecured overnight deposits, reported by a panel of contributing banks to the European Central Bank.

SONIA (Sterling Overnight Index Average) – this index is published by the London-based Wholesale Markets Brokers' Association. As with EONIA, Deutsche Bank carry out the daily compounding calculations to turn it into a total return index.

Federal funds effective rate – this is a reference rate (like LIBOR [London Interbank Offered Rate]), used in loan agreements. It is the annualised rate that equates to the rate charged in federal fund transactions among members of the US Federal Reserve System.

MTS is another European money market index publisher, which also operates electronic trading in Italian government bonds. It is 60% owned by Borsa Italiana, now part of the London Stock Exchange. The EuroMTS indices are not total return.

3. Currency ETFs

'Currency ETF' is an ambiguous term as currency ETFs are usually money market ETFs in foreign currencies. For example, WisdomTree launched several ETFs in early 2008 with names like WisdomTree South African Rand Fund, which were reported as being currency funds but were in fact cash funds.[98]

---

[98] In fact these WisdomTree ETFs were interesting for a number of reasons. They are supposed to give investors exposure to the dollar exchange rate for a number of individual currencies but not only were they not invested in those currencies but (for reasons of low liquidity in the countries in question) the securities they were invested in were US ones (short-term money market securities and forward currency contracts and swaps). Furthermore, these ETFs are among the first truly active ETFs (see Chapter 7).

By contrast, Rydex Investments' CurrencyShares Euro Trust is a US-domiciled fund set up (in 2008) to give US investors exposure to the euro rather than to earn income. Not surprisingly, all the euro bought to make up creation units in the fund are put to work earning interest, which is used to pay the fund's expenses. What is left over is paid to the ETF's shareholders on a monthly basis with the income payments based on EONIA. Although a currency ETF such as CurrencyShares will perform much like a euro money market ETF, its primary purpose is quite distinct.

Among sponsors of ETFs domiciled in Europe, ETF Securities developed its range of pure currency ETFs in 2010. These currency ETFs are based on Morgan Stanley Foreign Exchange indices. These are total return indices, giving investors exposure to the spot exchange rate between the long and short currencies in the pair (for example, ETFS Long Australian Dollar – Short British Pound) and differences in money market rates for the two currencies.

4. Credit ETFs

A credit ETF is one that tracks a credit derivative index. These indices track the cost of buying protection (in the form of credit default swaps [CDSs]) against the possibility of bond issuers defaulting.

References to credit ETFs can be ambiguous. State Street Global Advisors launched a range of ETFs that the press covered with headlines like "State unveils long-term credit ETF". In fact the ETFs' full names were SPDR Barclays Capital Long Term Credit Bond ETF, SPDR Barclays Capital Intermediate Term Credit Bond ETF and so forth. These were bond ETFs.[99]

Of course, likelihood of default is a crucial yardstick in setting bond prices so credit ETFs are closely related to fixed-income ETFs. Indeed, investment in a credit ETF can be one way of implementing a shorting strategy for fixed income assets. For example, at the time that General Motors filed for bankruptcy on 1 June 2009 it was reckoned that the event would trigger pay-

---

[99] These ETFs were not a State Street/Barclays joint venture, but were sponsored by State Street and tracked indices compiled by Barclays.

outs on $2.33bn-worth of credit default swaps to GM bondholders who had insured their investment in this manner.

Credit ETFs, by this definition, would normally be the preserve of institutional investors, but European ones are UCITS III compliant. The main sponsors of credit ETFs are db x-trackers and EasyETF. These ETFs are swap-based.

Among European-domiciled ETFs the best known credit ETFs are probably db x-trackers iTraxx Europe, iTraxx Europe HiVol and iTraxx Europe Crossover, which were all launched in 2007.[100] There are also short or **inverse** versions of these ETFs. iTraxx Europe tracks the performance of an index of credit default swaps for investment grade bonds for 125 European companies. iTraxx Europe HiVol tracks the credit default swaps of 30 of the most volatile components of the iTraxx Europe index, while iTraxx Europe Crossover tracks an index of credit default swaps for 50 of the highest yielding European corporate bond issuers. EasyETF also sponsors funds for each of these three indices.

5. Property ETFs

Property ETFs are usually taken to mean ones that are tracking indices for real estate investment companies and real estate investment trusts (REITs), of which the leaders are DJ Stoxx 600 Real Estate TR Index and the FTSE/EPRA (European Public Real Estate Association) property indices. The main sponsors of European-domiciled property index ETFs are iShares and Easy ETF. Although European investors are able to select property ETFs by world region, the range does not yet run to offering a choice of property types.

This kind of property ETF is only slightly removed from ordinary sector ETFs. A type of property ETF that is just beginning to appear and which represents quite a different kind of opportunity are ETFs that aim to track a property price index.[101]

---

[100] iTraxx is a brand of the International Index Co. Ltd.

[101] See 'Short property ETFs', in chapter 6.

Chapter 5

Exchange Traded Commodities (ETCs)

Exchange traded commodities, also called **commodity ETFs,** track the price of a specific commodity or a general commodity index (see following box for clarification on terms). They are regularly in the top ten exchange traded instruments by turnover and by number of trades on the London Stock Exchange.[102] For example, the second most traded ETF on the London Stock Exchange is the Lyxor Gold Bullion Securities Ltd gold ETF, and the ETF Securities ETFs in physical gold, natural gas and leveraged crude oil all occupy places in the top ten most traded ETFs.

Bearing this in mind, it appears that exchange traded instruments have done more to open up commodity investing than any other development in the investment industry – they have made the process of commodities investing both much easier and more akin to equity investing.[103] Nevertheless, there are important differences between ETCs and equity ETFs that should be kept in mind:

- It is possible to invest in a single-commodity ETC. Clearly, there is no place for the single company ETF – the investor would simply buy the shares – but individual commodities are more difficult to invest in than individual shares, so an ETC for a single commodity makes plenty of sense.

- ETCs track commodity indices, and these indices are very different to equity indices.

- ETCs are created differently from any of the methods of creating ETFs (and consequently the risks to the investor are somewhat different).

- The regulatory position of commodity ETFs is slightly different to that of exchange traded funds.

---

[102] Exchange Traded Funds and Exchange Traded Commodities: Monthly Statistics, (**www.londonstockexchange.com/statistics/specialist-issues/etfs-etps/etfs-etps.htm**).

[103] Both equity ETFs and ETCs are open-ended investments that are traded like shares on stock exchanges. Their sponsors tend to market them in similar ways: They appear side-by-side on their websites along with their fact sheets and prospectuses.

Commodity ETFs and exchange traded commodities

The terms 'commodity ETF' and 'exchange traded commodity' are often used interchangeably. The separate classification, 'exchange traded commodity', was more or less invented by the leading European player, ETF Securities, which launched the first ETC in 2003. Some European institutions, notably the London Stock Exchange,[104] Bloomberg, Reuters and the Deutsche Boerse, have followed ETF Securities' lead while most European sponsors continue to refer to 'commodity ETFs'. This book will follow the LSE and use the term ETCs.

In North America a distinction is sometimes drawn between commodity ETFs (meaning ETFs tracking equity indices of raw material producing companies) and commodity futures ETFs (meaning ones that track commodity futures indices). One subtle distinction between a European ETC and a US commodities futures ETF is that the former will replicate by means of swaps whereas the latter will normally track its index by in-kind replication.

From the next chapter of this guide onwards statements about ETFs should be taken to cover ETCs as well unless it is stated that they only apply to equity ETFs.

Exchange traded funds for precious metals

Although ETF Securities coined the phrase 'exchange traded commodity', its first ETC, Gold Bullion Securities,[105] came closer to an in-kind equity ETF than some other ETCs have done. The reason for this is that precious metal

---

[104] The London Stock Exchange created an exchange traded commodities trading platform in mid-2006. To date, all the ETCs listed there have ETF Securities as their issuer.

[105] Gold Bullion Securities is an ETC that has had a rather confusing history owing to the fact that its marketing was in the hands of Lyxor ETF from 2005 to October 2008, at which point it reverted to ETF Securities. During this period the ETC was known as Lyxor Gold Bullion Securities. To further complicate matters ETF Securities is also the sponsor of ETF Securities Physical Gold. Both Gold Bullion Securities and ETF Securities Physical Gold have their primary listing in London and can be traded on the Frankfurt, Paris and Milan exchanges.

ETCs tend to be 100% backed by the physical metal (in a vault in places such as London, Zurich, or Perth in Australia). In some cases it is also possible for authorised participants in the ETC to use physical metal for the creation of fresh units. This is similar to the way that actual index constituent shares are used in the full in-kind replication model for creating fresh units in an equity ETF. Normally, where physical delivery is an option for creating new units, authorised participants will have the alternative of paying cash instead. Zuercher Kantonalbank (ZKB) is another precious metal ETC issuer that permits delivery of physical metal in the ETC creation process.

Gold ETFs

Table 5.1 – Top three gold ETFs listed on the London Stock Exchange with trading volumes and asset figures

ETF	Trading turnover average[106]	Asset figures (millions)[107]
Lyxor Gold Bullion Securities Ltd	16,104,044	£2,590
ETFS Physical Gold	8,248,425	£2,240
ETFS Gold	950,365	£80

In addition to gold the other precious metals available as ETCs are silver, platinum and palladium.

Precious metal ETCs, traded on exchanges in the European Union and where the security is fully backed by the physical metal are normally UCITS' compliant.[108]

---

[106] Over 100 days to 10 February 2010.

[107] Figures are approximate for mid-February 2010 and converted from dollars into sterling at the exchange rate at the time.

[108] The UCITS' compliant status of precious metal funds is not straightforward. UCITS' rules appear to exclude funds that acquire precious metals or certificates representing ownership of precious metals (Simmons & Simmons 'ETFs Regulatory Framework; EU' 2010) so it is unclear on what basis a gold ETF is UCITS' compliant.

The storage factor

The reason that precious metal ETCs can be physically backed is that the storage costs are so low in proportion to the value of the commodity. The annual storage costs of gold, for example, to 0.01% of the value – compared to, for instance, oil, where the annual storage cost would probably be over 20%.[109] Thus storage factors add an extra dimension to commodities futures investing. This is not always explicit in media coverage of the subject, which tends to serve the needs of professional commodity traders rather than other types of investor.

Single-commodity ETCs, apart from precious metal ETCs, will track indices that track the price of futures contracts for the commodity concerned.[110] They will be backed by a credit agreement and collateral.

ETCs tracking single commodity indices

An examination of ETCs that track single commodity indices is key to understanding ETC construction.

Although tracking an index is a simple enough principle, commodity indices (for both single and multiple commodities) are calculated in an entirely different way to equity indices. The basic conundrum for the indices (and the ETCs) is how to construct an ongoing price figure from fixed-term futures contracts. The answer to this puzzle is to have the futures contract **roll on** to a different futures contract when the life of the future draws to its end.[111]

Let's look at this solution in the context of the commodity crude oil. The ETC in this example is ETF Securities Crude Oil,[112] which tracks the DJ-UBS Crude

---

[109] 'The Deutsche Bank Guide to Commodities Indices', July 2007.

[110] This is a slight simplification in that it is possible for a single commodity ETC to track the price of the relevant futures directly. For example, the giant United States Oil Fund tracks the price of West Texas Intermediate light crude futures directly.

[111] Although ETCs are the most important class of exchange traded product to track indices based on futures contracts, it is possible to design exchange traded products for other asset types that work in a similar fashion. For example ETFs have recently been developed that track indices of futures contracts for stock dividends. Similarly, Morgan Stanley's currency indices are based on forward currency contracts.

[112] The convention of including the title of the index being tracked in the name of the ETF breaks down in the case of single commodity ETCs.

Oil Sub-Index (a subset of the Dow Jones-UBS Commodities Index), which in turn tracks the prices of the NYMEX (New York Mercantile Exchange) crude oil futures contracts.[113] The roll-on process is illustrated in Figure 5.1.

Figure 5.1 – The roll on of the Dow Jones-UBS Oil Sub-Index

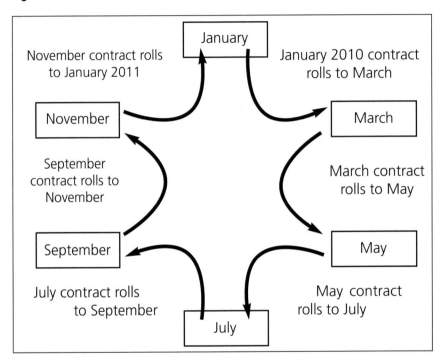

ETC contract roll on example – based on the ETF Securities Crude Oil

The DJ-UBS Commodities Index tracks energy futures contracts that deliver[114] in the odd months of the year and rolls on between the 5th and 9th days of the month (for example, in February the March contract will be rolled to the May contract). Other indices may track monthly futures contracts and roll forward on a monthly basis.

---

[113] This was formerly known as the DJ-AIG Crude Oil Sub Index but AIG (American International Group) sold its commodity index business to UBS in January 2009, including rights to use the Dow Jones-AIG index and sub-indices, a range of commodity index swap products. The name of the family of indices, of which the sub oil index is a part, was changed to DJ-UBS.

[114] Each futures contract is labelled according to the delivery month.

The problem with tracking prices through futures contracts

Each *roll on* from one contract to a later one represents a real transaction that the ETC has to make – quite regularly there will be a step up or a step down in contract price. The problems of tracking a commodity by means of futures contracts will show up in the changes in the relevant index. The ETC will track its index adequately but the index will not be tracking the spot price of the commodity in question. This has implications for the performance of ETCs and merits close attention.

The difference between tracking an equity index and tracking a commodity index (or the underlying futures contracts) is that shares in an equity ETF represent a fixed proportion of the index being tracked but an ETC share is invested in futures contracts. In a rising market the price of an ETF's shares simply follow the index up, but at contract roll on in a rising market an ETC is not able to afford as many futures contracts as it was able to at the previous roll on.

Funding the roll on of the futures contracts could cause a decline in the share price of the ETC at a time when the price of the commodity in question is rising. Certainly, it should be assumed that an investment in an ETC will give the return that the headline rises or falls in the price of the underlying commodity might suggest. ETC sponsors do set out the effect that rolling on has on an index in some detail in their prospectuses,[115] so this situation should be made clear.

For a crude oil ETC such as that of ETF Securities, the roll on transactions look like this:

---

[115] The investment and risk considerations section of the ETF Securities' prospectuses are especially helpful in this regard.

Example of contract roll on for crude oil

In December the ETC buys a March futures contract that puts the price of oil at $35 a barrel.

Two months later it must off-load this contract.[116] This oil is worth more than it was two months ago (the market is rising) and the contract fetches $40 a barrel. The ETC has made a profit on this phase of the roll on.

However, the price of the May futures contract is $48 a barrel. Even though the ETC made a profit on the sale of the previous bi-monthly contract, it is able to reinvest in less oil in February than it could in December.[117]

Figure 5.2 shows the typical process of formation for an in-kind replication ETC based on commodity futures contracts. Note that commodity futures markets are normally leveraged; investors in commodity futures only put up 5% to 15% of the cost of the futures as margin. This means that around 90% of the cash generated by the ETC in the primary market is used as collateral and as such is invested by the commodities market exposure provider. A swap-based ETC – all European Union-domiciled ETCs are currently swap-based – would be formed in a similar way to a swap-based equity ETF (see Figure 3.3).

---

[116] How this is done depends upon the exchange. If the ETC did not sell, it would have to take delivery of the crude oil.

[117] Of course, if fresh funds have flowed into the ETC, it will be able to buy more than that. In the case of an ETC with very large assets the problem could be even worse with the sale of the current contracts depressing their price and the purchase of the next set of futures contracts inflating their price. The US Commodities Futures Trading Commission investigated this possibility in relation to the US Oil Fund (assets $3.35bn) in February 2009. More recently, the financial media have also focused on the likelihood that some traders are anticipating and exploiting ETCs' need to roll on to the next month's futures by buying them up just before the roll date in order to sell them to commodity futures index trackers at a higher price.

Figure 5.2 – Creation process for an ETC

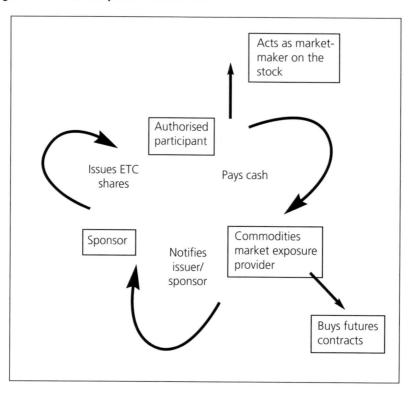

Futures contracts in contango and backwardation

In cases where the commodity futures prices are progressively higher the further ahead the maturity date is, the market is said to be in 'contango'. This is the situation described in the example above.

If, however, the commodity futures prices are progressively lower, the further ahead the maturity date is, the market is described as being in 'backwardation'.

If the commodity is in contango, the ETC investor will earn a negative roll yield. Conversely, when the commodity is in backwardation the roll yield will be positive.

Futures contracts should not be confused with forward contracts, which are traded over the counter in non-standard quantities.

Methods for solving the problems caused by rolling contracts

There are ways for ETCs tracking commodity indices to modify the effect that rolling on has on their performance. One relatively simple solution is, instead of a fund being wholly invested in a single period's futures contracts and being rolled on to the next period's futures contracts, the holdings can be spread across a greater number of time periods. An example of an ETC that follows this approach is the US 12 Month Oil Fund, which spreads its holdings across the next 12 monthly futures contracts.[118] The drawback with this approach is that, if a commodity's futures market swings from contango to backwardation, the advantage swings back to rolling on to the nearest month's futures contract in the conventional manner.

A further refinement in handling roll on effects is to *choose* which futures contracts to roll on to with the aim of maximising the advantage when the futures market is in backwardation or minimising the disadvantage when it is in contango. This means that the index or ETC rolls on to the cheapest futures contract even if this is not the nearest one. This approach is taken by the Deutsche Bank Liquid Commodities Indices Optimum Yield (DBLCI-OY). db x-trackers have one London-listed ETC tracking this index, their DBLCI-OY Balanced ETF. There is also a DBLCI-OY ETC traded on the NYSE Arca, and Powershares also has eight more tracking sub-indices of the DBLCI-OY.

Source ETF, one of the newest European players, has introduced another method for preventing roll on from eating into ETC returns. Its Source S&P GSCI Crude Oil Enhanced T-ETC uses an index that can switch each month between a front month and a six-month futures contract depending on how steep the futures curve is.

Another way around the problem is achieved by the UBS Bloomberg Constant Maturity Commodities Index. Constant maturity is achieved by rolling on a proportion of the contracts every trading day. This index and its sub-indices are tracked by ETCs traded on the SIX exchange in Switzerland.

---

[118] The debate about the performance of ETCs has been conducted overwhelmingly in the US with US Oil Fund often cited as an example of the problem and the US 12 Month Oil Fund as an example of one solution.

In late 2009 a further refinement to ETCs was unveiled by SummerHaven Investment Management. The SummerHaven approach is not merely to mitigate the effects of roll on when commodity futures are in contango but to develop commodity futures indices that seek to avoid contango before it occurs. The claims made for the SummerHaven Dynamic Commodity Index are based on research carried out by the company's founders[119] and published in a paper called 'The Fundamentals of Commodity Futures Returns' in 2007. The key finding of this research was that low inventory levels for a commodity are predictive for phases of backwardation. The United States Commodity Fund has agreed to sponsor an ETC tracking the SummerHaven index.

It should be noted that these strategies are designed to find ways around the losses caused by negative roll yield; they don't necessarily track the spot price of the relevant commodity any better than an ETC tracking the front month futures contract. A novel way to imitate spot price performance might be to use ETFs tracking a miners' or an oil companies' sector index or an ETF tracking the currency of an oil-producing country, such as the Norwegian krone.

The components of ETC returns

The price of the ETC reflects both the spot price of the commodity and the roll-on price of the futures contracts. The only scenario that would allow the index to track the spot price of the commodity fully is the – unlikely – event of a succession of futures contracts changing in price in exactly the same proportion and direction as the spot prices.

There is one further source of return for an ETC, which is the interest earned on the collateral (otherwise known as the **collateral yield**). Futures contracts are all traded on (futures) exchanges and the exchange acts as a central counterparty for all the futures positions. Futures exchanges use a margin

---

[119] SummerHaven was founded by K. Geert Rouwenhorst, Gary Gorton and Kurt Nelson. Rouwenhorst and Gorton were the authors of the landmark 'Facts and Fantasies About Commodity Futures (2004). The authors of 'The Fundamentals of Commodity Futures Returns' were Rouwenhorst, Gorton and Professor Fumio Hayashi.

system for payment and the initial margin is typically in the range of 5-15% of the value of the contract. The remainder of the ETC's funds can be invested, normally in government paper, and this generates another stream of return for the ETC. **Total return** commodity indices are ones that include the collateral yield in their calculation.[120] ETF Securities, the main European ETC sponsor, tracks total return indices.

There is no collateral yield in the case of precious metal ETCs as the investment is (or should be) fully backed by bullion.

ETCs tracking broad commodity indices

The main publisher-compilers of broad commodity indices are:

- Reuters-Jeffries/CRB Index (RJ/CRB) – this began as the CRB in 1957 as an index tracking spot price and switched in 2005 to tracking rolling futures

- Standard & Poor's Goldman Sachs Commodity Index (S&P GSCI) for which data goes back to 1970

- Dow Jones-UBS Commodity Index (DJ-UBSCI) – this index was launched in 1991, and alongside the S&P GSCI is considered to be a benchmark in the field of commodities investing

- Deutsche Bank Liquid Commodities Indices (DBLCI), which was launched in 2003

- Lehman Brothers Commodity Index

- UBS Bloomberg Constant Maturity Commodity Index.

---

[120] Some commodity indices that are not total return (and the ETCs that track them) refer to themselves as 'excess return'. One example is ETF Securities' Agriculture DJ-UBSCI ETC. This is a very specific kind of excess return and does not really equate to excess return when it is taken to mean over and above the risk-free rate of return. Investors would be well advised to read up on the indexing method of any ETC they are considering with some care as sponsors do not use descriptions such as 'excess return' and 'total return' in a uniform way.

Differentiation between the different commodity index publishers is based on roll-on mechanism, constituents and weighting. There is no key principle – an equivalent of cap weighting in equities – to serve as an anchor in the field of commodities investing.

The S&P GSCI weights constituents according to the relative value of production over the preceding five years, whereas the DJ-UBSCI is weighted primarily according to liquidity factors, but with production values being a secondary factor. The Rogers International Commodity Index (RICI – established in 1998), which is the broadest of all, weights according to international trade data on the 36 constituents.

The practical effect of these differences in weighting formulae is to give the different commodity indices wide variations in the proportion of the index that is made up by energy-related items. This is important because the weighting afforded to energy commodities is often regarded as being key to the profitability of exchange traded commodities or commodity funds. Historically, the tendency of energy futures markets to be in backwardation has been the main contributor to returns in broad commodity indices.

Table 5.2 – Proportions of indexes that are compromised of energy-related items

Commodity index	Energy component[121]
S&P Goldman Sachs	71%
Deutsche Bank Liquid	55%
Rogers International	44%
Reuters-Jeffries/CRB	39%
Dow Jones – UBS	34%
UBS Bloomberg	33%

With broad index ETFs, it should be remembered that an index may have different roll-on mechanisms for different commodities. Thus, while rolling on of oil futures contracts may be done on a monthly basis, the roll on for agricultural commodities or industrial metals could be annual.

---

[121] The energy constituents of these and other indices vary but the most common are West Texas Intermediate (WTI), Brent crude, gasoline, natural gas, heating oil and gas oil.

Index strategies for good returns from ETCs

Momentum – commodity indices have been developed that attempt to build in an automatic response to signals that a particular commodity's futures market is moving from backwardation to contango. The index then shorts the relevant commodity to avoid negative roll yield until the reverse signal is picked up – that contango is giving way to backwardation and it is time to *go long* the commodity. This strategy depends on periods of contango or backwardation enduring for several months at a time.

Examples of indices reflecting this kind of sophisticated momentum strategy are the Morningstar Long/Short Commodity Index and Standard & Poor's Commodity Trends Indicator. It is worth noting that neither of these indices ever short energy futures; Morningstar switches from energy futures to cash and the S&P index switches into other commodities.

This is a more sophisticated version of momentum than the weighting by production levels kind used by the S&P GSCI.

European ETCs that track these momentum indices have yet to appear.

Mean reversion – as an alternative kind of rebalancing, Deutsche Bank has developed indices in which the constituent commodities are rebalanced in response to significant changes in the price of any one of them, with a significant upward movement in the price of a commodity causing its weighting to be reduced.

Deutsche Bank also compiles a mean reversion plus index, which balances the broad commodities spectrum against cash (represented by US Treasury bills), comparing the performance of the two types of asset in each of the 12 preceding months and allocating funds accordingly.

The mean reversion and mean reversion plus strategies would be employed where returns on commodities are not expected to correlate amongst themselves or where commodities as an asset class are not expected to correlate with government debt. In other words, mean reversion works if one particular commodity is in a speculative bubble but not if all commodities are in a bubble. A mean reversion plus strategy gives protection from the effects of a speculative bubble affecting all commodities but it won't work if speculation is driving government bond prices too high simultaneously.

ETCs and regulation

The subject of exchange traded commodities and compliance in the European Union has become confused. This is partly because single commodity ETCs and broad index ETCs are permitted by some national regulators (such as those in the UK) and can be used for an ISA (individual savings account) or SIPP (self-invested personal pension) even though they appear to flout UCITS III requirements in relation to investment concentration.

The reason this situation has developed is that European domiciled ETCs are UCITS III eligible investments, not UCITS III compliant funds. That means that UCITS III compliant funds can invest in them, not that they are UCITS III funds in themselves. One simple check is to look to see if the product sponsor has provided a simplified prospectus, which is a requirement for UCITS III compliant funds and so an ETC will not have such a document.[122]

However, one important safety feature has appeared since 2008. Many of the non-energy ETCs sponsored by ETF Securities were backed by futures contracts with AIG Financial Products. During the financial crisis in 2008 trading in many such ETCs was suspended as investors became worried about counterparty risks involving AIG (the funds invested in the futures contracts only had to be collateralised by AIG in the event of its Standard and Poor's credit rating falling below BBB+). As a result, AIG now fully collateralises its obligations with regard to the funds invested on behalf of these ETCs.

UCITS non-compliance by other ETCs is not universal. For example, Deutsche Bank's Liquid Commodity Index, Optimum Yield Balanced, and iShares' Dow Jones-AIG Commodity are both UCITS III compliant. Significantly, both of these products are referred to as ETFs by their sponsors, and both are swap-based with the swap comprising a basket of equities.

At present European domiciled ETCs do not replicate commodities indices in-kind. However, this method of replication is used by US commodity futures ETFs. In these cases the ETF has counterparty exposure to the commodities exchange, as commodities exchange trades all work with a central counterparty (the exchange itself). The main commodities exchanges all have the highest credit ratings.

---

[122] Under UCITS IV the simplified prospectus will change to a document entitled 'Key Investor Information'.

The risks of investing in ETCs

- There are a variety of different structures of ETC that track different things:

  - Physical ETCs hold the physical commodity on an investor's behalf and track the spot price.

  - There are ETCs that track the futures price of a single commodity.

  - ETCs are also available that track the price of an index comprised of the futures prices of a basket of commodities.

There are also inverse and leveraged ETCs, which adds extra complication and risk.

With the exception of physical ETCs, ETCs do not track the spot price of the commodity or the price of futures contracts in the commodity, in the way that equity ETFs track the price of an equity index. This is because of the effects of contango and/or backwardation.

The popularity and growth in range of ETCs is one major manifestation of the new wide-scale interest in commodity speculation. It's too soon to predict the long-term effect on commodity assets of mass involvement by the investing public.

The difference between an ETC and an exchange traded note (ETN)

The AIG counterparty risk in some of ETF Securities' ETCs was dealt with rapidly and effectively. Investors in three Lehman Brothers' exchange traded instruments were less fortunate. These were **exchange traded notes** marketed under the Opta brand: the Commodity Index Opta ETN, the Commodity Agriculture Opta ETN and S&P Listed Private Equity Index Opta ETN.[123]

ETNs are similar to ETCs and ETFs in that all three trade on exchanges and have returns that are related to indices. The difference with ETNs is that they are debt instruments and the investor is fully exposed to the risk of a default by the issuer; investors do not own a slice of any underlying commodities futures or equities. In the event of the issuer's bankruptcy, the investors are treated in the same way as other creditors.[124]

Although commentators were warning about the credit risks associated with ETNs well before the bankruptcy of the Lehman Brothers, problems in distinguishing between ETCs and ETNs could still be caused by the misuse of the terms themselves. Even sponsors refer to their ETCs as having a *note structure* and some media coverage fails to distinguish between ETCs and ETNs at all.

---

[123] ETNs are not limited to just commodities; emerging market equities, currencies and investment strategies such as options can all be tracked by this means.

[124] However, it is possible to have a collateralised ETN such as Lyxor's gold ETN. In fact, Lyxor have gone one stage further and made the collateralisation an add-on. The total expense ratio is increased to those investors who elect to have the collateralised version of the note.

Summary

The level of research required before investing in commodities ETFs may be a factor that discourages their wider use; not only do the workings of commodity indices need to be mastered but there are multiple market forces to be gauged. One of the attractions of ETFs is that they save time and/or money because less research and effort is needed for individual stock picking. However, with commodities ETFs time has to be spent doing homework and then ETC investments need to be watched closely – a *buy and hold* strategy would not be appropriate.

The one type of ETC that is relatively straightforward is precious metals ETCs, where the underlying investment is physical bullion.

Chapter 6

Advanced ETFs:
Further Refinements to the ETF Model

So far this guide has explored the ETF universe across the broad asset categories – equities, fixed income, property and commodities. This chapter looks at refinements to ETFs that are modelled on less straightforward approaches.

With advanced ETFs several of the key features of the ETFs already covered in this guide may be modified or missing altogether. For instance, advanced ETFs do not reduce risk by tracking broad indices and there may be a lack of transparency about what exactly the constituent parts of an advanced ETF's creation unit are. The most dangerous sacrifice of all is the loss of simplicity – in other words, the understanding of how the ETF works.

Advanced ETFs, such as those that imitate hedge fund performance or those that are active investments, certainly merit examination but it is important also for the basic attractions of ETFs to remain on the investor's checklist. For a reminder of key attributes of ETFs, see pages 17-18 and the summary on pages 123-124.

This chapter will look at the following types of advanced ETF:

1. leveraged ETFs

2. short ETFs

3. **active ETFs**

4. ETFs that imitate hedge funds

5. private equity ETFs.

It is worth noting that ETF categorising is particularly contentious in these advanced areas. For example, leverage is part of the stock in trade for hedge funds, so a hedge fund ETF will involve some kind of leverage.

Almost without exception these advanced types of ETF are new or very new. Consequently, in some cases the only examples of a particular type are US-based, rather than ones domiciled within the European Union. Although nothing is sure in the development of investment products, it is reasonable to assume that most, if not all, of these advanced products will spread beyond the US within one or two years.

1. Leveraged ETFs

Leveraged ETFs aim to multiply the effect of changes in the price of an asset. For example, in the case of an X2 leveraged ETF tracking the FTSE 100 share index, a rise in the index of 1% on a given day would cause a 2% rise in the price of a share in the ETF. Conversely, a 1% fall in the index would lead to a 2% fall in the price of the ETF's shares. With an X3 leveraged ETF a 1% rise in the index would result in a 3% rise in the price of the shares in the ETF. There are leveraged ETFs available in both Europe and the US.

In Europe:

- Lyxor sponsors leveraged ETFs for the CAC 40 and the DAX, in both cases doubling the exposure to these indices.

- Somewhat confusingly, the asset management arm of Lyxor's parent Société Générale, SGAM, also had a leveraged ETF for the CAC40 (now merged with its Lyxor twin) as well as one for the FTSE Eurofirst 80.

- XACT Fonder sponsors the XACT Bull, which provides leverage of 1.5 times the Swedish large cap index.[125]

- ETF Securities sponsors leveraged versions of most of its ETCs.

In North America, Direxion, Proshares and Rydex are the most prominent sponsors of leveraged (and short) ETFs. The US Securities and Exchange Commission only sanctioned leveraged ETFs in 2006.

Leveraged replication is normally achieved by various combinations of investments in the equities of the index being tracked, futures contracts, swap agreements, forward contracts and **options**. Overall, the largest proportion of replication for leveraged ETFs is achieved by means of swaps, both for European- and US-domiciled ETFs.

---

[125] In 2005 XACT Fonder was the first to sponsor leveraged and inverse ETFs.

Risks of leveraged ETFs

Most sponsors caution that the real effects of leveraged ETFs need to be considered carefully. For Direxion, the caution is even in the name of the individual ETFs, as in 'Daily Large Cap Bull 3x Shares'; these ETFs can only accurately leverage the movements of their indices on a day-by-day basis. It is the percentage rises and falls that are leveraged and this can have unexpected effects. Consider, for example, the compounding effect of an ETF that returns 200% of the day-by-day fluctuations on a volatile index:

Table 6.1 – The effect of leverage in an ETF over two days in a volatile index

	Plain long ETF	Leveraged ETF (X2)
Day one +10%	starts 4000 ends 4400	starts 4000 ends 4800
Day two -12.5%	-550 ends 3850	-1200 ends 3600
Net decline	3.75%	10%

Far from coming right in the end, leveraged ETFs can demonstrate some remarkable divergences from their indices, even ending up down when the index is up. ETFs giving leverage on a day-by-day basis have their uses but providing a hedge for long-term investments is not one of them. As the table of London-listed ETFs with the highest trading volumes shows (see page 22), some ETCs, such as ETFS Leveraged Crude Oil, do indeed have disproportionately high trading volumes considering the size of their assets. This suggests that they are being used for frequent trading.[126] Volatility will work against leveraged funds over the longer term, while non-volatile market conditions and strong trends will tend to work in their favour.

---

[126] Nevertheless, some sponsors of leveraged ETFs do still recommend very long minimum investment terms.

2. Short ETFs

A **short ETF** is an ETF that aims to deliver inverse returns to the index it is tracking. This means that if the FTSE 100 index rose by 2.5% on a given day, the value of an inverse FTSE 100 ETF would be designed to fall by 2.5%. Conversely, if the FTSE 100 fell by 5%, the inverse FTSE 100 ETF should rise by 5%.

The first European-domiciled short ETF, the XACT Fonder's XACT Bear, was not only short but leveraged (by 1.5 times) as well. Sponsors of European-domiciled short ETFs include db X- and EasyETF, in addition to those sponsors of leveraged ETFs listed above. Short (inverse) ETFs tend – like leveraged ETFs – to use swap-based replication.

Risks of short ETFs

Short ETFs do not necessarily track the inverse of the index's performance *over long periods of time*. Owing to the same compounding effect that we saw in relation to leveraged ETFs, in volatile conditions inverse ETFs are not able to inversely track their indices closely. Leveraged short ETFs will suffer the same divergence effects as those of leveraged ETFs, but in an even more pronounced manner. An example is provided in Table 6.2.

Table 6.2 – The divergence of short ETFs from the performance of the index they track

	Plain long ETF	Inverse performance	Short ETF
Day one +10%	starts 4000 ends 4400	-10%	starts 4000 ends 3600
Day two -12.5%	-550 ends 3850	+12.5%	450 ends 4050
Net decline	3.75%	Net rise	1.25%

Short ETFs ran into problems in the latter part of 2008 when regulations were introduced in several countries (including the US, the UK, Australia, Belgium, France, Germany and Japan) to prohibit shorting of stocks, especially financial stocks. In some cases this caused severe tracking errors for short ETFs as investors continued to buy the ETFs on the secondary market while the shorting ban prevented creation units being assembled to create more ETF shares to meet the demand.

In addition to short or inverse ETFs, it is also normally possible to engage in shorting strategies with long ETFs. It was reported that stock-lending (presumably for shorting purposes) of iShares FTSE 250 ETF amounted to 50% of the ETF's shares in January 2008.[127]

Investing in short ETFs as opposed to other shorting strategies

The advantage that short ETFs have over shorting strategies in general is that with short ETFs, unless the investor leveraged themselves to buy the ETF shares, the risk is limited to the size of the investment; the ETF share can fall to 0 but no further. By contrast, ordinary shorting strategies can potentially expose the investor to the risk that the price of the asset that has been sold short will rise without limit.

Short property ETFs

Some commentators have pointed out that in regions like the British Isles and the Iberian Peninsular – where there have been bubbles in residential property prices – short ETFs may well be the solution to a perennial problem. With so much of so many people's personal wealth tied up in their homes, there has traditionally been a lack of means for investors to express negative sentiment about house prices.

In the US this looked to be changing with the advent of the MacroShares Major Metro Housing Up and its obverse, the MacroShares Major Metro Housing Down. The former tracks the S&P/Case-Shiller house price index for ten major US cities and the latter tracks the inverse of the index.

---

[127] Robert Mackinlay, 'FTSE 250 short selling falls to pre-credit crunch levels', *The Financial Express*, 15 May 2008.

In the event these two ETFs failed to generate enough interest and were closed down at the end of 2009. However, Royal Bank of Scotland was expected to launch a *house price bear product* in 2010. The details of exactly how this would work and whether or not it would be exchange tradable have yet to be revealed.

A UK equivalent of the MacroShares exchange traded products, using index data from the Halifax, Nationwide or the Land Registry would provide a convenient way for householders to back a negative hunch about house prices if, say, they were planning a move abroad or downsizing. Conversely, people saving to buy a house might consider investing in the long version of the property ETF if they feared that house prices were going to run ahead of returns from any other kind of investment.

The MacroShares ETFs were three times leveraged, which increases the risk of the investment itself but reduces the outlay when purchasing the ETF. Even so, a lot of the short ETF shares would be needed to hedge against the possible fall in value of a whole house.

3. Active ETFs[128]

There is some question over what exactly qualifies an exchange traded fund as active and how active ETFs actually work.[129]

An active ETF can be defined as being one that is "managed by an investment adviser who uses his/her judgment to select stocks in an attempt to outperform the market."[130]

---

[128] Also sometimes referred to as 'intelligent' ETFs. However, 'intelligent' in the context of ETFs can be a very broad category, covering anything from trackers of non-cap-weighted indices to the genuinely active ETFs and all points in between.

[129] The workings of an advanced ETF is important intellectual property for its sponsors and sometimes for associated index compilers. In some cases, even stock exchanges are claiming intellectual property rights for changes to their procedures to support the trading of advanced ETFs. None of this bodes well for the ordinary investor who wishes to look 'under the bonnet' before they decide to buy these products.

[130] Neal Wolkoff, American Stock Exchange.

The criterion of routine human interventions in the ETF's strategy is essential. Judged by this definition, truly active ETFs are evidently not passive and do not include any ETFs whose investment changes result purely from programming (even if the precise changes depend upon elaborate contingencies).

This description of a truly active ETF excludes far more so-called active funds than it includes. In particular, the need for an active investment adviser rules out much of the class of what is becoming known as **quantitative-active ETFs**.

Quantitative-active ETFs have been around since 2005 and have been described as:

> "Rules-based ETFs that are effectively trying to add to an index return through a statistical sorting of some type. The 'active' in quantitative-active stems from the fact that the index – and therefore the ETF – reconstitutes its holdings on a monthly or quarterly basis depending on the results of the latest sort."
>
> **Scott Burns, Director of ETF Analysis, Morningstar, August 2008**

Examples of quantitative-active ETFs are Invesco PowerShares' Dynamic Large Cap Value ETF and Dynamic Mid Cap Growth ETF, and the First Trust AlphaDEX family of ETFs in the US. Powershares also has a Dynamic US ETF listed on the London Stock Exchange. Until 2009 there was also the range of SPA MarketGrader ETFs for sale on the London Stock Exchange and the Borsa Italiana.[131]

The anatomy of a quantitative-active ETF

Like ETFs tracking fundamentally weighted or style-based indices, quantitative-active ETFs aim to beat the broad cap-weighted indices. The difference between a quantitative-active ETF and an ordinary fundamentally weighted or style-based ETF is that the index for a quantitative-active ETF

---

[131] The SPA MarketGrader range of ETFs, which began trading in 2007, applied for delisting from the exchanges with effect from 1 May 2009. The reason given was market conditions. All six of the SPA MarketGrader ETFs had experienced falls of over 25% in the 12 months to 1 March 2009. At the time of the funds' closure SPA said that it may reintroduce the MarketGrader strategy at some future date.

will always have more selection criteria and will combine two or more approaches. For example, PowerShares' Dynamic Indices combine 25 factors in all, including fundamental criteria, timeliness,[132] risk factors and stock valuations. For the Dynamic Large Cap Value ETF, stocks are also filtered by market capitalisation and then further filtering (involving ten more tests) is applied for the appropriate style. The stocks are not only selected but scored so that PowerShares can produce what it calls an 'investment merit ranking', which decides what stocks go into the ETF and what weighting they have.

The First Trust Large Cap Value Opportunities AlphaDEX Fund seeks to track a custom-built index called the Defined Large Cap Value Opportunities Index, compiled for First Trust by Standard and Poor's. The index combines pure value stocks and others that are more value- than growth-oriented according to S&P's criteria.[133] The presence of value stocks that have some growth characteristics explains the opportunities element in the index name. At first glance this ETF may look like just another style-based offering but in reality it is definitely a new take on style.

Both these quantitative-active ETFs are rebalanced on a quarterly basis.

Truly active ETFs

The group of truly active ETFs is currently tiny. Increase in numbers is likely to come partly from quantitative-active ETF sponsors who add a degree of human intervention so that what would be a quantitative-active ETF shades into a truly active one.

In the case of PowerShares' Active Alpha Q and Active Alpha Multi Cap Funds there is no custom-built index[134] but these ETFs do apply a proprietary stock-screening methodology. Just how much of the methodology is automatic

---

[132] Timeliness in this context is a proprietary methodology based on intensive research for comparing US companies to see whose time has come. The methodology and the 'Timeliness' trade mark are the property of Value Line Publishing Inc. of New Jersey.

[133] S&P uses a similar system to that used for its own style indices (see example in 'Definitions of style' box on pages 30-31.

[134] Although truly active ETFs will not normally track an index, they will have benchmark indices that they seek to outshine.

and how much discretion the investment manager has remains unclear, but the funds' fact sheets do state that there is some management risk.

The first truly active ETF

The first truly active ETF was the Bear Stearns' Current Yield Fund which began trading on 18 March 2008, a couple of days after the buyout of the company by JP Morgan. The fund was invested in fixed-income instruments and its brochure said that it had the potential to provide higher returns than money market funds *and* that returns would depend upon the effectiveness of its portfolio management team. The three main areas where active management would come into play were:

1. analysis of the macroeconomic environment

2. sector allocation

3. research for the selection of securities.[135]

Portfolio disclosure

An important question for active (and quantitative-active) ETFs is whether, and if so, how, they achieve transparency in relation to their creations and redemptions. The dilemma for the sponsors of an active ETF is that full, timely disclosure would inevitably mean that other investors might take advantage of the information about the portfolio that they were making public. Acting on portfolio information in this way is known as **front running**, but this sort of copycat tactic is not usually pursued in relation to information that is in the public domain.

In the case of Bear Stearns' Current Yield Fund the sponsor opted to provide full transparency. The other truly active ETFs are WisdomTree's currency income funds. These funds are designed to give exposure to certain foreign currencies in US dollar terms and achieve this aim by investments in currency contracts, repos, government bonds, treasury bills, corporate bonds,

---

[135] The fund also weighed the distribution of its securities in terms of maturity to make the most of the yield curve, but it is not clear if this part of the strategy was executed according to human judgement or according to rules decided upon before launch.

commercial paper and the money market (all entirely within the US). Information about the holdings of each fund is published daily in the normal ETF fashion. Creations and redemptions are made using a specified basket of foreign currency and dollars.[136]

The consensus is that active ETFs investing in equities or longer maturity fixed-income securities will desire less than total disclosure of their holdings.[137] There are a number of theories as to how this might be done but these remain speculative in the main. Possibilities include:

- A proxy portfolio that approximates to the real portfolio and can be used for creation and redemption purposes. Authorised participants would be able to make their arbitrage calculations on the basis of the proxy portfolio.

- A black box or scrambler solution whereby the net asset value of fund constituents is made public but their identity remains confidential. It seems that the American Stock Exchange (AMEX) had been working to develop solutions of this kind and that the NYSE is continuing their development.

- Two tier disclosure; full disclosure for authorised participants to facilitate the creation and redemption processes with less disclosure to investors in the secondary market. The Vanguard Group has suggested that this would be very unfair to the investing public.[138]

- The simple stratagem of timing portfolio changes to make it awkward for competitors to take advantage of the information. In the case of

---

[136] Bear Stearns Current Yield Fund also allowed cash (as opposed to in-kind) creations and redemptions.

[137] However, the Grail American Beacon Large Cap Value ETF, which launched in the US in May 2009, claimed to be the first fully active qualitatively managed ETF *and* promised full portfolio disclosure on a daily basis. At roughly the same time iShares launched an active equity ETF and an active fixed-income ETF with full portfolio disclosure the day after any portfolio changes. At the time of writing it was not yet clear whether front running would be a problem for any of these funds.

[138] Comment letter sent by Vanguard Group to the SEC, February 2002.

Powershares' Active Alpha Q and Active Alpha Multi Cap the fund manager only makes changes to the portfolio late on Fridays so the altered portfolio is only made public the following Monday morning.[139]

So far all active and quantitative-active ETFs in the US have satisfied the Securities and Exchange Commission that they are acting in a fully transparent fashion in relation to their portfolios.

The lone European active ETF sponsor

At the time of writing the sole European active ETFs were the range of ETFs originally sponsored by Société Générale Asset Management, using the SGAM brand rather than the Lyxor one. This range of ETFs was absorbed under the Lyxor brand in late 2009.

The first selling point of SGAM's flexible range of three ETFs is that 80% of the share price on 31 December of the previous year is guaranteed. These are, therefore, ETFs with a built-in floor (although more than 20% of the original investment can be lost if the ETF is bought when the benchmark index is higher than it was at the end of the previous year and the index then declines by more than 20%).

The active element in SGAM's strategy is the changing view taken by the funds' managers on the likely trend of the relevant index. In anticipation of bearish conditions, the ETFs will reduce exposure and invest the funds in the money market instead.

---

[139] There seems to have been a measure of confusion about Powershares' creation/redemption basket requirements. Despite the fact that the ETFs' portfolio is fully disclosed on the Invesco Powershares' website, some commentators suggested that there would be problems in fully replicating the portfolio and that the basket would only be similar to it. This approach looks akin to the proxy portfolio solution but it is difficult to see why that should be necessary since the sponsor is disclosing the portfolio in full. The prospectus for these active ETFs is slightly ambiguous; saying at one point that the creation basket must be made up from stocks in the universe of the individual ETF but later on refering to "substantial replication" of the actual portfolio.

The three ETFs currently in the flexible range are for the CAC 40, the DJ EURO STOXX 50 and the FTSEurofirst 80. Management fees at 0.5-1% are higher than average for ETFs.

SGAM also have leveraged ETFs, bear ETFs and combined leveraged bear ETFs, where again their managers intervene to reset exposure to the market on the basis of their analysis. In the case of these ETFs they are not truly pure leveraged or pure inverse ETFs but ones where exposure is up to a certain percentage of the underlying index. However, as the name suggests, SGAM's Private Equity ETF gives full exposure to the LPX 50 (Leipzig Power Exchange) private equity index.

4. ETFs that imitate hedge funds

ETFs designed to imitate the most active funds of all, hedge funds, are not yet a full reality. Currently, mention of hedge fund ETFs can be referring to a number of distinct fund models and several different approaches are outlined below.

Hedge index tracking

Hedge fund index tracking follows the typical ETF approach: an index of funds is chosen and then replicated by the ETF. There are not many ETFs taking this approach yet, but one example is the Credit Suisse Tremont Hedge Index, which goes back to 2003.[140]

The problem with this approach is that investable hedge fund indices only comprise a small fraction of the total hedge fund universe.[141] Consequently, only a fairly small portion of hedge fund indices can be tracked in this way.

---

[140] The minimum stake for this type of investment is normally far higher than for shares in an ordinary mutual fund or an ETF.

[141] The number of hedge fund indices was put at 30 in 2007, of which nine were investable. Martin Steward, 'The thorny problem of how to classify a hedge fund index', *Financial Times*, 2 July 2007.

The Credit Suisse Tremont Hedge Index is one of the largest investable indices but only includes about 5% of the total number of hedge funds.[142] Furthermore, there is no agreement as to whether hedge fund indices should be equally weighted, weighted by assets or a combination of both.

A fund-of-funds approach

This is really tracking hedge fund indices by another name. Regulatory and other constraints would make it difficult to sponsor an ETF that selected hedge funds on an active basis.

Mimicking hedge fund performance through other ETFs

This is a new strategy developed by IndexIQ with its IQ Hedge Multi-Strategy Tracker ETF. IndexIQ have created an index that reflects six different hedge fund strategies. However, the ETF is not invested in hedge funds but in a combination of other ETFs that in aggregate will, IndexIQ's analysts believe, perform in a very similar fashion to the index. This ETF was launched in 2009 and is quoted on the NYSE Arca exchange. It is too early to say how well its strategy of investing in other ETFs will enable it to track its index. Most attention has so far been paid to the novelty of using ETFs to replicate hedge fund investments rather than fund managers' discretion in selecting the ETFs. Although in theory this fund is tracking an index, this looks more like a fully active ETF, albeit one that invests in passive funds and discloses its portfolio in full.[143] The ETF has a relatively high expense ratio (to which must be added the expense ratios of all the ETFs that it invests in), and partially relies on leveraged and inverse ETFs.

---

[142] That is 500 out of 10,000. Deborah Brewster, 'Hedge fund indices compete for attention', *FT* Special Report on Index Investing, 3 November 2008.

[143] Although IQ Hedge Multi-Strategy ETF is passive in as much as it tracks an index, the mechanism for tracking investment in other ETFs appears to depend exclusively on the skill of the managers. The prospectus clearly states that the possibility that the managers might fail is one of the ETF's risks. It seems surprising that this has not drawn more comment. The registration filing with the SEC says that the ETF "employs a 'passive management' – or indexing – investment approach designed to track the performance of the underlying index". It goes on to say: "The Fund invests primarily in the underlying index components that make up the underlying index." (Securities Act File No. 333-152915; Investment Company Act File No. 811-22227.) Presumably this investment in the underlying components of the index has to be taken in a very general sense.

A managed account approach

This is an approach pioneered by db x-trackers with the launch of its db Hedge Fund Index ETF on the Deutsche Boerse's XTF market segment in March 2009, tracking the eponymous index. Hedge funds are retained to advise a number of mutual funds set up by Deutsche Bank in Jersey, each mutual fund representing a different hedging strategy. The investment funds raised by the ETF are invested across these mutual funds. This looks like another instance of a significant active ingredient in the form of the advisors' discretion[144] in the management of the mutual funds. It's not clear how much attention they have to pay to the index the ETF is supposed to be tracking, or what the regulators will say if the advisors miss the target.

London Stock Exchange-listed sterling and dollar versions of this ETF were launched in July 2009.

5. Private equity ETFs

Due to the nature of private equity – companies being controlled through holdings of shares that are not listed on a public exchange – there is no direct route into private equity for ETFs.

Examples of ETFs that specialise in this area are iShares S&P Listed Private Equity (i.e. publicly listed funds that invest in private equity) and Powershares Listed Private Equity Portfolio, which tracks the Red Rocks Capital Listed Private Equity Index, an index of the stocks of 30 US companies which in turn have stakes in over 1000 unquoted companies between them.

---

[144] db x-trackers have taken care to ensure that their index covers several different hedging strategies. The db Hedge Fund Index captures the performance of the dbX Tactical Index Hedge Fund family. The allocation of the assets of the ETF to the different hedging strategies is according to distribution of assets across strategies for the hedge fund industry as a whole (with quarterly rebalancing). In some ways this looks like the most ambitious attempt to square the active strategy/full transparency circle to date.

PART THREE:
Investing In ETFs

Chapter 7

ETF Practicalities

This chapter will look at investing in ETFs from a practical point of view and will cover the following subjects:

1. how ETFs can be used

2. what to know about an ETF before investing

3. sources of ETF information

4. broker considerations

5. when to trade ETFs

6. how often to trade ETFs

7. regulation, custody and taxation

8. when an ETF is shut down.

This list leaves out the related questions of where to start with ETF investing and how far to take it. Ultimately, these are questions of personal taste and/or investing philosophy but one particular approach to investing is provided at the end of this section.

1. How ETFs can be used

Exchange traded funds, in common with all collective investments, have the advantage of diversification: of spreading an investment further and reducing the risk. In addition they are excellent instruments for tracking indices. Other uses for ETFs as an investment class include:

- **Diversification into equities in other regions or industries** – The performance of foreign or new markets can be tracked through region or sector index ETFs.

- **Diversification into various asset classes** – ETFs are available for equities, currencies, commodities and bonds, as well as more advanced areas.

- **Sector rotation** – Moving in and out of different industrial sectors through the economic cycle becomes easier with ETFs.

- **Balancing an existing portfolio** – The diversification of a portfolio can be improved easily by investing in ETFs covering areas that do not include existing holdings.

- **An alternative to a large cash balance** – Those with temporary large cash balances can speedily switch into (and out of) a suitable ETF.

- **Harnessing the skills of fund managers and other analysts** – Someone can appreciate the usefulness of picking stocks by growth criteria or according to fundamentals without necessarily having the knowledge or inclination to make the selection themselves; tracking a value index or a fundamentally weighted one with an ETF solves this problem. This point was made by Burton Malkiel, author of *A Random Walk Down Wall Street*, in 2007. Specifically, he suggested that economic forecasters or commodity experts might use ETFs to invest in shares without having acquired the skills of an investment analyst.

- **Short and leveraged investments** – **Short ETFs** and **Leveraged ETFs** make it possible to earn higher but riskier returns by using some of the strategies used by hedge funds.

None of these uses of ETFs are without risk. An investment in, say, the FTSE Rafi Eurozone may produce better results than efforts at stock-picking continental European companies, but it will not provide protection from an abrupt fall in the value of the euro. The benefit is in the range of possible investments that ETFs open up. Although there are additional risks in branching out into new asset classes or investment strategies, at least ETFs make these options available.

2. What to know about an ETF before investing

The main points that need to be researched for each ETFs are:

1. the replication model

2. the index and possible problems with over-concentration

3. (likely) tracking difference

4. (likely) liquidity

5. (likely) spreads

6. expense ratios

7. its currencies

8. regulatory status (UCITS' compliance)

9. taxation status.

This may seem like a lot of bases to cover but, compared to many investments, a good ETF should be transparent. However, there are three facets of ETFs in particular that can produce complications and which merit extra attention. These are:

1. the danger of inadvertent over-concentration in particular assets

2. the effect of exchange rates on one's ETF returns

3. potential liquidity problems of an ETF.

These will be investigated more thoroughly in Chapter 9.

3. Sources of ETF information

Most of the relevant information for ETFs can be found on the internet. The key places to hunt for the information are:

The sponsor's website – some sponsors' websites are very good (iShares, for example). The key items to look out for are:

1. The *fact sheet*. This will provide information about the index being tracked, regulatory compliance, trading volumes, assets under management, exchange listings, market-makers and, hopefully, a brief description of what the ETF does. The fact sheet should also provide, at a glance, vital information about whether or not an ETF is UCITS III compliant, if it can be included in an ISA[145] or a SIPP, and the fund's **distributor status**.[146]

2. The *prospectus*, which will provide vastly more detail. Look here for information about the replication model and the various types of risk the ETF is exposed to. Confusingly, some sponsors publish a single prospectus for all of their ETF offerings. The prospectus often looks unmanageably large but, generally speaking, they have a clear table of contents. European Union UCITS' compliant sponsors should provide short prospectuses with condensed information.

3. The way in which the website *categorises the sponsor's range of ETFs* should give a clear idea of the type of ETFs being offered (for example, ETFs may be differentiated by country equity and regional equities, or fixed income; ETCs may be listed separately from equity ones).

4. It is also worth looking out for helpful *marketing materials* explaining the sponsor's overall approach to their ETF businesses.[147] db x-trackers and iShares provide useful **correlation** matrix tools so that the degree of correlation in returns between various leading indices can be seen.

---

[145] Most London-listed ETFs can be included in an ISA but money market ETFs can only used for the cash component of an ISA.

[146] Distributor status (or, since 2009, **reporting status**) for investment funds is an HMRC designation allowing investors in a fund to treat capital gains as such rather than paying income tax on the capital gain. Most London-listed ETFs have distributor status but most of iShares' range of property ETFs are an exception.

[147] iShares and db x-trackers are especially helpful in this regard among European ETF sponsors.

Financial information providers – Online services provided by Bloomberg and Thomson Reuters have invaluable free charting facilities. These can be very useful for monitoring how well an ETF tracks its index. The brief descriptions provided about indices and instruments can also be a handy check on one's understanding of the information provided by the ETF sponsors. Especially useful is the up-to-date information on premiums or discounts to NAV, bid/offer spreads and assets under management.

Stock exchanges – As well as being the best place to check for an exchange listing for a specific ETF, websites such as that of the London Stock Exchange are the best place to compare ETF share price movements during the trading day. Regulatory announcements about net asset values – issued each day – also provide information about the number of shares in issue. Checking back over recent months' announcements should enable one to build up some idea of the amount of creation and/or redemption activity.

Media comment – There is a steady flow of articles about ETF investing in the personal finance pages of newspapers. *Money Observer* is beginning to cover ETFs in more detail and for over a year has published monthly price data for most of the ETFs domiciled in the European Union. Coverage in the *Investors Chronicle* is also growing.

Specialist information providers

- Index Universe (**www.IndexUniverse.com**) is the best resource for European ETFs. This website has a European correspondent (see **www.IndexUniverse.eu**) and it is also excellent for US coverage.

- Seeking Alpha (**www.seekingalpha.com**) sends out *ETF Daily*, an e-letter compilation of relevant articles. It is also good for the US.

- The ETF section on Morningstar (**www.morningstar.com/Cover/ETFs.aspx**) has good information on US exchange-traded products. Morningstar have launched an ETF Centre with a UK focus in the last year and now publish a monthly newsletter on UK ETFs.

- Another specialist is **www.etfzone.com**, but it tends to focus on North America exclusively.

- The *Financial Times* has a dedicated resource for exchange-traded products on its website (**www.ft.com/uk/ftfm/etfs**).

Taken together these resources provide an invaluable source for debate on ETFs and act as a counterweight to what the sponsors themselves have to say.

Online brokers/fund supermarkets – Most online stockbrokers are beginning to offer ETFs and provide lists of the full range across sponsors with helpful background data. Some providers offer useful portfolio analysis tools which are invaluable in providing, for example, a breakdown of investment holdings by geography or by industry.

The difficulty of finding information

Unfortunately a lot of sponsors' documentation is clearly aimed at meeting legal and regulatory requirements rather than offering assistance for those trying to find out more about the fund. It can be very difficult to nail down the true character of an ETF.

Take, for example, the question of how the ETF is put together; is it by full in-kind replication or swap-based replication? An ETF's prospectus will not normally make this matter entirely clear. Typically, the sponsor of an ETF with in-kind replication will be anticipating circumstances where that method of replication runs into difficulties. So they give themselves reserve powers to replicate the index by some other means, should that contingency arise, such as allowing cash creations and redemptions.

Although prospectuses may not provide *all* the necessary information on an ETF, they can provide useful pointers. For example, a prospectus may not say, in so many words that the ETF is active but, if, among the list of risk factors, it mentions management risk, it is likely that there is an active ingredient in the fund's workings.

It is a good idea to complement the sponsor's documentation by reading up elsewhere too.

Searching for an ETF

An ETF's name will normally be constructed in the following order:

1. The sponsor's brand name (e.g. iShares or Lyxor ETF).

2. The name of the index being tracked; although in the case of exchange traded commodities this will usually be replaced by the commodity itself. Do not be confused by sponsor's names popping up as the index compiler for another sponsor's ETF.

3. The ETF's symbol or ticker. For example, the IQ Hedge Multi-Strategy Tracker ETF has the ticker QAI while db x-trackers FTSE 100 ETF has XUKX. These are normally three or four characters long and are useful for searching for information about the ETF; commentators often use them as shorthand for the full name and they are usually very much easier to remember.[148] The ticker will be followed (or on some information services, preceded) by a one, two or three letter exchange identifier. For example IUSA is an iShares ETF tracking the S&P 500 and its London listing is specified as IUSA:LN. To complicate matters, tickers can be quite different for secondary listings if the primary listing ticker has already been taken by another stock on the stock exchange where the secondary listing occurs.

---

[148] Ticker symbols have not been used so far in this guide but are included from this point onwards. These are all London-listed ETFs unless another exchange is specified. However, all ETFs mentioned in the text are indexed with their ticker. In the UK the correct name for a ticker is a Tradable Instrument Display Mnemonic (TIDM), having been formerly known as EPICs.

4. Broker considerations

ETF shares cannot be purchased through the ETF sponsor and so a broker is needed.[149] Facilities for trading ETFs vary between online stockbrokers.

The most important subject relating to a stockbroker and ETF investments is the proportion of the total range of ETFs and ETCs that they allow investors to trade in. Some online brokers make this key information easily accessible on their websites.

Other questions to ask of brokers include:

- Can investments in ETFs be made through an ISA?

- Can investments in ETFs be made through a SIPP and, if so, is there an annual management charge that is different to that for other forms of collective investment or holdings of individual stocks?

- Are the dealing charges for ETFs exactly the same as for dealing in individual stocks?

- If an ETF has liquidity problems or high bid/offer spreads, it may be important to place **limit orders** when buying or selling – does the broker make this option available?

- Is it possible to buy an ETF that has a foreign currency as its trading currency?

Hargreaves Lansdown and Selftrade are two services that are more open than most about the options available to their clients as far as ETFs are concerned. TD Waterhouse's service gives access to US-domiciled ETFs for those who sign up for its international equities service and Interactive Brokers also facilitates ETF trading on North American and some continental exchanges. ETF prices and charting are available from most brokers who include ETF dealing in their service, but in-depth information about individual ETFs has to be sought elsewhere.[150]

---

[149] Although in countries where shares are normally bought and sold through retail banks ETF investors will often be using the services of a bank whose investment arm happens to be an ETF sponsor.

[150] Selftrade does provide links to the websites of major European ETF sponsors, a convenient refinement.

The duplication of ETFs among European stock markets, with numerous sponsors bringing out their own versions of a DJ EURO STOXX tracker, has been a focus of attention in the media. However, using a broker that permits dealing in ETFs listed on foreign stock exchanges would allow a UK investor to buy, for example, ETFs tracking the DAX or the CAC40 indices; currently there is no listing for ETFs tracking either of these on the London Stock Exchange.

5. When to trade ETFs

There has been some evidence from the US that ETFs can be slow to begin trading after the market opens and that, consequently, the index tracking may not be quite as effective in the first half hour of the trading day.

In the case of ETFs that are tracking overseas markets, some commentators recommend trading the ETF when the market of the underlying asset is open for trading. The reasoning behind this insight is that market-makers are happier quoting prices for the ETF when the underlying asset is being traded, which results in better liquidity and spreads. As a counter-argument it could be suggested that, if liquidity is that much of a problem, the ETF is best avoided.

---

db x-trackers facilitates trading at NAV

Institutional investors have had the option to buy and sell ETFs at the end of day net asset value. The main advantage of this tactic is that they avoid the drain to profitability of paying for the market-maker's spreads. The main disadvantage of the approach is having to wait until the end of the trading day for the trade to be executed.

db x-trackers has extended the option to purchase or sell ETFs at NAV to other investors. It comes with an extra charge on top of normal dealing charges, of between 0.03 and 0.30%, depending on whether the ETF in question tracks developed market equities or emerging market ones.

However, in the event of severe liquidity problems on an emerging market's stock exchange, the investor will still be exposed to the danger that the NAV itself could become very volatile.

---

6. How often to trade ETFs

The tradability of ETFs – it is possible to trade ETFs all day – is an advantage since ETFs can be traded into and out of when the need arises. However, there is a danger that too much use will be made of this tradability and as a result ETFs will become frequently traded rather than held for the long term. In other words, whereas the best investment approach might be to trade very occasionally, with ETFs it is tempting to trade frequently resulting in investment returns being eroded by brokers' commissions and bid/offer spreads.

For example, there is evidence to show that ETF investors as a group are achieving poorer returns than the ETFs themselves by trading them too frequently and timing their portfolio changes badly. Advocates of passive mutual funds, such as John Bogle, point to this evidence and use it to argue that all-day tradability of ETFs is not a strength but a serious weakness.

In truth, there is no single right answer to the question of how frequently to trade ETFs. Like single company shares they can be used for strategies involving very frequent or very rare trades, or trading that fluctuates between extended periods of holding ETFs and occasional portfolio overhauls. The trading frequency that is best might depend upon the type of ETF being invested in, for example whether it is an equity ETF, ETC or advanced leveraged/short ETF.

The logic of holding *ETFs that track equity or fixed-income indices* seems to be to treat them as long-term investments but, although timing market peaks and troughs is notoriously difficult, a buy and hold approach that takes no account of financial and political headwinds can lead to setbacks too.

ETF types that are not suited to being held for the long term

As explained in previous sections, ETCs tracking futures indices are one exchange traded product that does not seem suitable for long-term investments. In addition, leveraged and inverse ETFs are designed for frequent trading and may give unexpectedly poor returns if held for longer periods.

The investment periods in which the divergence of leveraged ETFs from their indices becomes problematic is a complicated subject. Leveraged ETFs (and inverse ETFs) tend to do what they are supposed to over a single day and over a period of less than a week divergence should not be too marked. However, a leveraged ETF left unattended for a month or more could be dangerous. Trading volumes for leveraged and inverse ETFs are a much bigger proportion (27% in April 2009) of the total ETF trading volumes than their share of total ETF assets (6%), which suggests that many holders of leveraged ETFs know not to hold them for very long.

7. Regulation, custody and taxation

Regulation

Although UCITS III compliance counts for a lot, there are a few extra considerations to bear in mind:

1. No amount of regulation in the ETF's home country will protect holders of ETFs that have foreign assets against unjust treatment in these other jurisdictions. In fact, this is one area where ETF prospectuses come into their own, many making a very competent job of describing foreign jurisdiction risks.

2. Just as with investments in ordinary equities, those investing in ETFs should check how much protection they have if their ETF shares are held in nominee accounts (in other words, they are only the beneficial owners) and their stockbroking service was to go out of business.

3. ETF sponsors will normally have to abide by regulations in two different jurisdictions. Firstly, the regulator in the country in which the ETF is domiciled will have a hand in how the ETF is marketed and promoted. Secondly, the stock exchanges on which the ETF is traded will enforce their own rules in this area. For example, many ETFs listed on the London Stock Exchange will be domiciled in the Republic of Ireland. For ETFs such as the iShares FTSE 100, this means they will be regulated by the Irish regulator and will abide by the London Stock Exchange rules. Also, as a UCITS III fund, they will have to abide by UCITS' rules too.

4. With regard to ETF regulation itself, it is useful to monitor the indices ETFs are tracking. In the EU, the main concern of regulators has been to check that neither the index tracked nor the replication method lays the

ETF open to too great a concentration in one or more assets. There does not appear to have been the same attention given to the performance of indices in providing objectivity, capturing realistic prices and generally coping when liquidity disappears.

Custody

Although ETF investments do not have legal protection from investment and counterparty risk, it is unlikely that they could be exposed to outright fraud. As we have seen, a fund's promotion and share trading are taken care of by the regulators. The fund's assets are held in custody for the shareholders in the fund;[151] there is no danger that the ETF shares can become mixed up with any other investment activity carried out by the sponsor or its parent company.

The structure that each sponsor uses for their ETFs may vary. For example, db x-trackers' ETFs are legally sub-funds of a single fund. In the case of iShares the structure is that of a series of companies (iShares, iShares plc, iShares II plc, iShares III plc, iShares Inc. iShares Trust) each with a number of (segregated) funds under their management. Lyxor ETFs are separate mutual funds with Lyxor International Asset Management as fund manager of each. The important principle is that the assets and expenses of each ETF are entirely separate from the assets and expenses of any other ETF issued by the same sponsor.

Taxation

For UK taxpayers there are two areas where ETF taxation may turn out to be unexpectedly complicated.

1. The **reporting status** (formerly known as distributor status) of the fund. This is important because it will affect the taxation of capital gains. Under the distributor status regime taxpayers were liable to income tax on all of the returns of a fund investment unless any income (from dividends or premiums) was distributed. This meant that they had to declare any capital gains as income and pay income tax on it. The reporting status regime operates in a similar manner but allows the income stream of a fund to be rolled into the total return of the fund (but it is deemed to be income and taxed as such).

---

[151] They may be used by the sponsor in a stock-lending programme; in which case the loaned stock should be fully collateralised.

2. Income from ETFs domiciled outside the UK (and almost all of them are) may need to be entered on the foreign pages of an HMRC tax return;[152] it is a simple process to download the right forms from the HMRC website. More seriously, ETFs domiciled in some jurisdictions may be subject to foreign withholding tax. In the case of ETFs traded on the London Stock Exchange, French-domiciled ETFs are the main group of ETFs affected in this way and the rate of tax is 25%. Thus, a UK taxpayer who has invested in a London-listed ETF tracking an index of UK stocks can still find themselves subject to a foreign tax deductable at source. Furthermore, only three-fifths of this French tax can be offset against the UK's dividend tax, leaving a higher rate taxpayer with another 17.5% tax to pay on the ETF's dividend.

8. When an ETF is shut down

It is not easy to calculate how much ETF sponsorship costs the sponsor but clearly not all ETFs will attract sufficient interest for the expense ratios to cover these costs. In these circumstances the sponsor will consider shutting the fund down.

Once the sponsor has announced that an ETF is going to be shut down there are a number of special considerations for those who hold shares in the ETF. The most serious (and most unlikely) is that the creation/redemption process will go so badly wrong that a wide tracking difference will develop between the ETF and its index. For example, in the last few weeks of an ETF's life – in circumstances where the index was rising – there could be insufficient new creation units to track the index. At this time the ETF shares could take on a life of their own independent of the index they were supposed to be tracking.[153]

---

[152] Tax forms for 2009/10 allow for up to £300 of income from foreign-domiciled funds to be entered on the ordinary investment income page of a tax return.

[153] Something close to this scenario occurred in March 2009 when Credit Suisse decided to shut down three commodity tracking exchange traded notes and stopped issuing new ETN shares before the market was properly aware of the imminent closure. Elements MLCX (Merril Lynch Commodity Index Extra) Gold Index share price rose to more than ten times the net asset value (the gold price being tracked). Normally, adequate stock exchange announcements and stock exchange supervision of the market-making in an ETF in its dying days should prevent recurrences of this kind of problem.

Even orderly ETF shutdowns pose a couple of problems for the shareholders.

1. Shareholders are faced with the choice of selling their ETF shares and incurring dealing charges, or waiting for the liquidation and final distribution of cash to shareholders. If they opt for the latter alternative, they are certain to see a deterioration in tracking as the sponsor turns assets into cash.[154]

2. The sponsor is likely to deduct its costs from the value of the fund. Typically, the most expensive life-stage of an ETF for the sponsor is the initial listing. If these start-up expenses have not been recovered by the sponsor (through the management fees) when they decide to liquidate the fund they are likely to be charged to the fund at this stage. As ETFs in danger of shutdown are likely to be small ones, the damage to the value of the fund could be considerable in proportional terms.[155] This may seem unfair on those unfortunate enough to be holding the ETF shares at the time but shareholders in an individual company would probably fare worse if the company went into liquidation.

The possibility of an ETF being closed down by its sponsor is a reminder that investors in the ETF are shareholders in the fund rather than customers of the ETF sponsor. The chief warning sign for an ETF in danger of being shutdown would be a low assets under management figure. Some ETF commentators write occasionally on what are referred to as 'deathwatch funds', which are the ETFs they consider fall into the in-danger category.

---

[154] Of course, if the relevant index is falling, the switch into cash by the dying ETF could be a good thing for shareholders.

[155] When SPA closed its six MarketGrader ETFs in March 2009, there were divergences of the order of 10-15% of the relevant indices as closure-related costs were charged to the fund ('SPA Fund Closure Cost Investors Over 10% of NAV', IndexUniverse, 3 April 2009).

What does a shareholder in a swap-based ETF receive if it shuts down?

One example of the multi-faceted nature of ETFs can be seen with the swap-based replication model that is prevalent for EU-domiciled ETFs. The Lyxor ETF FTSE 250, for example, provides exposure to the FTSE 250 (the second band of the London Stock Exchange's main stocks – after the FTSE 100).

However, this is not quite the whole story. Another aspect of the ETF is to know what would happen if the sponsor was to decide to wind it up. What would be distributed to the shareholders – the swap or the contents of the substitute basket?[156] The answer is that in the event of the ETF being wound up the shareholders would receive their share of the substitute basket, which in the case of the Lyxor ETF FTSE 250 is described in the prospectus as a basket of international equities.[157]

---

[156] See the section 'UCITS lll, ETFs and swap counterparty risk' on page 62.

[157] The end-of-life scenario being considered here is an orderly winding-up due, for example, to a lack of investor interest in the fund. In these circumstances it would be reasonable to expect the sponsor to continue with swap agreements for the index exposure almost to the end.

Chapter 8

ETFs as Portfolio Building Blocks

This chapter will consider ETFs as building blocks within a portfolio and will cover the following three topic areas:

1. Investment concentration

2. ETFs and currencies

3. Liquidity

1. Investment concentration

With collective investments such as ETFs (or investment trusts or investment funds) exposure can be unwittingly concentrated in one region or sector as a result of making investments that overlap.

An example of this is provided by the FTSE 100, which has a high proportion of foreign-domiciled companies and a high proportion of commodity producers among its constituents. Even FTSE 100 members that are household names, such as HSBC (Hong Kong and Shanghai Banking Corporation), in truth can represent an overseas investment (51% of pre-tax interim profits in 2008 came from the bank's Asian operations compared to 40% deriving from Europe as a whole).

FTSE 100/South Africa: an example of inadvertent concentration

At the time of writing a £2500 investment in an ETF tracking the FTSE 100 would mean that the investor was investing just under £140 in the following four companies:

- BHP Billiton (Broken Hill Propietary) (2.66% cap-weighting in the FTSE 100)

- Anglo American (1.42%)

- SABMiller (1.19%)

- Old Mutual (0.26%)

Were another £2500 invested in the Lyxor FTSE JSE Top 40 South Africa ETF, this would represent an investment in these same four companies (along with 36 others) but the extent of the stake would be 42% of the ETF (or £1067). Overall, just under one-quarter of the £5000 invested would be concentrated in four companies.

Concentration can take many different forms. Another example might be combining an investment in ETF A, which tracks the DJ STOXX 600 banking sector, with ETF B tracking eastern European stocks. At first glance this strategy seems like sensible diversification: EFT A invests in banks in western Europe while ETF B invests in companies in the countries of what used to be the Soviet bloc. However, if the DJ STOXX 600 banks have lent heavily to eastern European corporates, the investor may have inadvertently concentrated their exposure to this part of the world.

The danger of concentrating risks instead of diversifying them does not only exist when choosing equity ETFs – it also applied to bond ETFs, ETCs or a combination of asset classes.

2. ETFs and currencies

Thinking about an ETF's currency is not necessarily straightforward as many ETFs involve more than one. Understanding the roles of these currencies is vital when it comes to appreciating the effects of exchange rate changes on holdings of ETFs.

Functions of currencies in ETFs

An ETF investor can come across currencies in four different functions:

1. trading currency

2. base currency

3.   index currency

4.   investor's domestic currency.

We will now look at each of these in turn.

Trading currency

Every ETF has a trading currency, the currency in which it is traded on a stock exchange. Many ETFs have more than one trading currency. This may be because different versions of the same ETF are listed on two or more exchanges (which is known as **cross-listing**).[158] So an ETF listed on the London Stock Exchange and Euronext might have sterling as its trading currency on the former and the euro as its trading currency on the latter. However, it is also possible for two versions of the same ETF to be listed on the same exchange, alike in every respect except that they have different trading currencies. An example is db x-tracker's MSCI Emerging Market TRN (Total Return Net) ETF, which has two versions listed in London, a dollar version (XMDD) and a sterling version (XMEM).

As Table 8.1 shows, terminology for the different types of ETF currency varies from one sponsor to another, but for consistency's sake this section will follow the lead of db x-trackers and ETF Securities in using *trading currency* to signify the currency an ETF's shares are priced in on the stock exchange.

Base currency

Although every ETF must have a trading currency, it is crucially important to appreciate that the currency in which the underlying assets of the ETF are denominated – the base currency – does not have to be the same as the trading currency. For example, db x-trackers DJ EUROSTOXX 50 (XESC) has sterling as its trading currency but the base currency of the ETF is the euro (because all the component companies of the ETF have their stock exchange quote in euro).

The trading currency is determined by the sponsor's sales and marketing strategy, whereas the base currency is the one that determines the value of an ETF.

---

[158] From a legal standpoint these variants listed on different exchanges may be the same fund but with two different exchange codes for the different trading currencies, two separate but similar funds, or two sub-funds.

As with trading currency, consistency is lacking between different ETF sponsors over the terminology used when referring to the currency of the underlying asset.[159]

Index currency

It is easy to assume that the base currency of an ETF will always be identical to the currency of the index that the ETF is tracking because much of ETF sponsor literature would tend to suggest that this is the case. This is misleading. It is perfectly possible for an index to be expressed in a different currency from the one that the index constituents are normally quoted in. For example, iShares MSCI Brazil ETF (IBZL) has sterling as its trading currency and the dollar as the index currency[160] so that it might appear that the foreign currency exposure is to the dollar. In fact, the underlying assets are in Brazilian reals and this is where the true exposure lies.

For a large majority of ETFs the index currency and the base currency will be the same. The possibility of the index currency disguising where the true exchange rate exposure lies is confined mainly to equity index trackers, but even here only about 20% of funds are affected.

In the case of ETCs tracking commodity indices there is much less likely to be a difference between the index currency and the base currency of the underlying assets. The underlying assets will be futures contracts, normally denominated in US dollars, and the indices are also normally expressed in dollars.

An ETF's NAV will be expressed in the index currency but the intraday NAV (iNAV) can be expressed in the ETF's trading currency.

As mentioned, ETF sponsors are not consistent in the terminology they use to refer to the various currencies associated with ETFs. Table 8.1 summarises this variance.

---

[159] iShares uses the term 'base currency' to denote the currency in which the net asset value of an ETF is expressed. This is not incorrect; one definition of 'base currency' is that used for measuring gains and losses in an international portfolio. This is most likely to be the same as the index currency, *not* the true currency of the underlying assets. However, 'base currency' also means the currency which businesses (the underlying assets) use for their own accounts and this is the meaning use in this book.

[160] iShares themselves refer to the base currency being the dollar in this instance (see note 161).

Table 8.1 – ETF sponsors' currency terminology

Sponsor	Term for underlying asset currency	Term for currency ETF is traded in
db x-trackers	Fund currency	Trading currency
ETF Securities	Base currency	Trading currency
iShares	Currency or currencies of the assets in the creation or redemption basket.	Fund currency on exchange
Lyxor	Doesn't differentiate fully but does refer to 'index currency' (see below).	
Powershares Global Funds	Base currency	Doesn't differentiate fully but fact sheets do give a recent closing price in what is in effect the trading currency.

Sponsors' websites and fact sheets also refer variously to 'benchmark currency' or 'index currency', or give net asset values or index performance.

On the London Stock Exchange website the currency used for pricing information for ETFs will be the trading currency. Announcements about the NAV of the ETF will be in the currency of the underlying asset (although sometimes a currency conversion of the NAV to the trading currency is also provided).

Investor's domestic currency

An investor's domestic currency is taken to mean the currency of the country the investor is domiciled in. For an investor living in the UK their domestic currency would usually be sterling, whereas the euro would be the domestic currency for a person living in France. Of course, every investor is different and some may have accounts in more than one currency.

Although there are plenty of ETFs that have sterling as their trading currency, it can be easy for sterling investors to buy ETFs with the dollar or the euro as their trading currency, almost without noticing. As part of their service, the investor's broker may allow their clients to buy and sell foreign-currency denominated ETFs even though the client only has a sterling account. In such a case, the client would, say, buy a dollar-denominated ETF, and the broker would convert the dollar transaction value into sterling and deduct the sterling amount from the client's account. (When the client sells, the process is reversed.)

Once the foreign-currency denominated ETF has been bought, its price and value may then be displayed in the client's portfolio in sterling terms alongside all the other sterling holdings of the client. However, it should be remembered that this price and value of the ETF is only the sterling equivalent (at a conversion rate set by the broker) of an asset whose actual price is in a foreign currency (e.g. dollars or euros).

Different brokers are likely to vary on how they handle ETFs that have a foreign currency as trading currency, so a broker's specific procedures should be checked before dealing with them.

Where does exchange rate exposure lie?

For any ETF investments, except those where the base currency of the underlying assets being tracked is the same as the investor's home currency, there will be exchange rate exposure.

For example, db X-tracker's DJ EUROSTOXX 50 ETF has sterling as its trading currency, and the euro as the index currency and base currency – all the index constituents are quoted in euro. For a sterling investor the returns start with the net effect of constituents' share price changes on the index but are combined with the change in the euro/sterling exchange rate since the ETF shares were acquired. Foreign currency exposure is always going to have some effect on the returns of such an ETF and this makes it a degree more complicated to interpret what is happening.

The danger is in misinterpreting the ETF's returns, assuming, for example, that the ETF's share price has risen due to the performance of the underlying asset when in fact a large part of the returns are the result of a more favourable exchange rate. In a case like this it may not be appreciated how vulnerable the investment is to a sudden reversal in the trend of the relevant exchange rate. Table 8.2 provides some currency permutations of ETFs to show where currency exposure lies.

Table 8.2 – A selection of the currency permutations that can be present in individual ETFs to show where the foreign exchange exposure lies

Underlying asset (base) currency	Index currency	Trading currency	Investor's domestic currency	Currency exposure	ETF example
£	£	£	£	None	db x-trackers Sterling Money Market ETF (XGBP)
€/£/other	€	£	£	£/€ and other European currencies for a proportion of the fund.	PowerShares FTSE RAFI Europe (PSRE) The index comprises just over 50% euro zone companies, 30% sterling and some Swedish krona and some Swiss franc, so exposure is complex.
€	€	£	£	£/€	Db x-trackers DJ EUROSTOXX 50 (XESC)
Rouble	$	£	£	£/rouble	Db x-trackers MSCI Russia Capped Index (XMRC)
Brazilian real	$	£	£	£/real	Db x-tracker MSCI Brazil TRN (XMBR)
Brazilian real	$	$	£	£/real	Db x-tracker MSCI Brazil TRN (XMBD)
Brazilian real	real	$	£	£/real	Lyxor ETF Brazil ibovespa/UK (LBRU)
$	$	$	£	£/$	ETFS Crude Oil (CRUD)

More on the trading currency of an ETF

The following points merit further emphasis in considering the trading currency of an ETF:

- The trading currency of an ETF may not be the same as the currency of the country in which the ETF has its stock exchange listing. As we have seen, this is not always apparent because the stockbroker may be exchanging the home currency of investors for the actual trading currency of the ETF.

- In some cases the sponsor may have two ETFs trading on the same exchange that are identical in every regard except for having different trading currencies. An example is ETF Securities' Gold Bullion Funds which are both listed on the London Stock Exchange, one in dollars

(GBSS) and the other in sterling (GBS). The important point to remember is that investing in Gold Bullion Fund Sterling does not mean that the foreign exchange exposure of investing in an underlying asset that is priced in dollars has been avoided. The main advantage of having an ETF with one's local currency as its trading currency is that you do not have to worry about the possibility that your stockbroker is using an unfavourable exchange rate when they convert your local currency for you.

- In instances where the sponsors offer an ETF with more than one trading currency, it is likely that one of the trading currencies will be the index currency. However, as we saw, there are indices such as MSCI Brazil Index where the index currency is not the true base currency. In these circumstances it should be remembered that the option to invest in a version of an ETF where the trading currency is the same as the index currency is not a way of avoiding exchange rate exposure.

Gauging the effect of exchange rate exposure

The combined effect of changes in the value of an asset priced in a foreign currency coupled with the exchange rate movements may not always be exceptional. However, it needs to be remembered that an ETF gives two kinds of exposure: the change in the asset's price in the currency it is denominated in (its base currency) and, secondly, fluctuations in the exchange rate between the base currency and the domestic currency of the investor. As mentioned above, sometimes the currency changes may have a greater effect on the ETF price than changes in the underlying asset prices.

If holding several ETFs whose underlying assets are denominated in one foreign currency and the exchange rate enters a volatile phase it is possible to end up with plenty of exposure to a single exchange rate instead of the diverse returns that were planned for. Dollar-denominated ETFs, in particular, can spring up in some surprising places.

Let's look at the likely performance of a sterling priced gold ETF (Table 8.3). Assume that the prevailing gold price was $900 an ounce, the sterling/dollar exchange rate was $1.40 (gold costing therefore approximately £643 an ounce), and each ETF share represents one-tenth of an ounce of gold so that the shares were purchased for £64.30 each.

Table 8.3 – The combined effect of asset price change and exchange rates on the returns of a gold bullion ETF

Gold price ($ per troy ounce)	Exchange rate (USDGBP)	ETF price in Sterling
1000	$1.70	£58.80
1000	$1.40	£71.40
1000	$1.20	£83.30
900 starting price	**Starting exchange rate $1.40**	**£64.30**
900	$1.70	£52.90
900	$1.20	£75.00
800	$1.40	£57.10
800	$1.70	£47.10
800	$1.20	£66.70

In Table 8.3 it can be seen that if the price of gold moves up to $1000 an ounce while at the same time the USD/GBP exchange rate moves down to $1.70 (i.e. the dollar *falls* to that level), our ETF experiences a significant fall in its price. Conversely, if the exchange rate stayed the same while the gold price moved up to $1000 an ounce the investor would have enjoyed a positive return.

Case study: Gold Bullion Securities (GBS, GBSS)

Figure 8.1 compares the performance of the dollar-denominated Gold Bullion Securities ETF (GBS) with the underlying price of gold for the period November 2007 to August 2009.

The chart appears to show only one line because the GBS ETF tracks the gold price very closely – an example of a tracker working well!

Figure 8.1 – Gold Bullion Securities (GBS) v. gold

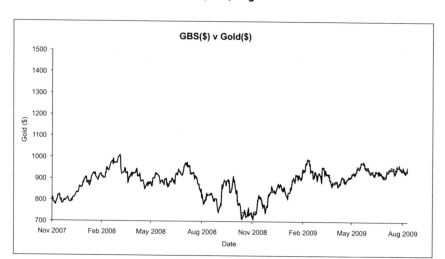

Now let's look at the sister ETF to GBS, the sterling-denominated Gold Bullion Securities ETF (GBSS). Figure 8.2 compares the performance of this ETF with the price of gold.

Figure 8.2 – Gold Bullion Securities (GBSS) v. gold

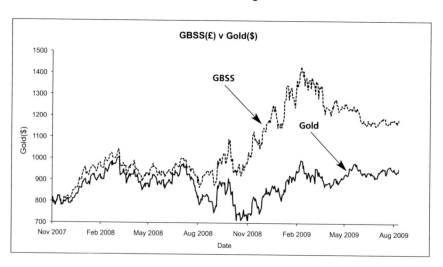

As can be seen, the GBSS ETF followed the gold price quite closely for about eight months from November 2007. This was because during this period the GBPUSD exchange rate did not change much (refer to Figure 8.3 to see that the exchange rate stayed around 2 for this period). But from August 2008, sterling fell sharply against the dollar. The impact on the GBSS ETF can be seen in Figure 8.2 – GBSS began to greatly outperform the gold price. The reason is that gold is priced in dollars, and the GBSS ETF rose in value reflecting the strength of the dollar against sterling. To put it another way, a sterling-based investor holding GBSS benefited because they were exposed to a dollar asset.

Figure 8.3 – Sterling/Dollar exchange rate

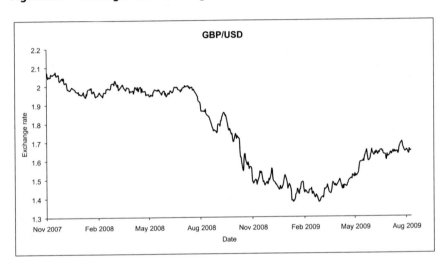

However, note that the return for a sterling-based investor holding either the Dollar GBS or the Sterling GBSS would have been the same. When the investor came to sell the Dollar GBS at that point they would benefit from the strong dollar against sterling. The investor in the Sterling GBSS also benefited from the exchange rate, but they gained day-by-day as the price of GBSS changed to reflect the exchange rate.

There is always the possibility that ETF sponsors may introduce ranges of ETFs tracking foreign underlying assets but where the foreign currency exposure is removed. This would give the investor pure asset returns. db x-trackers has launched a number of hedged ETCs.

The difference that exchange rates make to ETF performance is all the more complicated to keep track of if, as sometimes happens, investors receive price information about their ETF holding in sterling alongside prices and charts for the underlying in the original currency. Online brokers who combined charts of the performance of the ETF in the home currency of the investor overlaid with charts of the underlying asset in its currency would be providing a useful service.

When calculating exchange rate exposure can be especially difficult

Before leaving the subject of exchange rate exposure, it is important to realise that there is an even more insidious way in which this can creep into ETF returns. Earlier, we looked at the composition of the FTSE 100 in the context of inadvertently concentrating one's assets. Of course, an investment in the FTSE 100 also makes it possible to gain foreign currency exposure inadvertently. Even though the base currency of the Footsie ETF is sterling, as much as 60% of the earnings of Footsie constituents are in other currencies. Some constituents, such as Royal Dutch, even pay their dividends in another currency (dollars). So UK investors investing in the flagship UK index are already gaining plenty of foreign currency exposure by doing so. It would seem that foreign currency exposure is difficult to avoid even for the most conservative of investors.

Another important index that can cause similar headaches when it comes to understanding the currency exposure is the DJ STOXX 600, which is comprised approximately 50:50 of stocks that trade in euro and stocks that trade in other currencies (including sterling, Swiss franc and Swedish krona). ETFs that target regions or worldwide emerging markets are likely to come with multiple base currencies.

Fixed-income ETFs tend to be simpler than equity ones in regard to foreign exchange exposure. Fixed-income indices are all restricted to single currencies: The individual bonds that make up the index will all be in the same currency, which means that the base currency and the index currency will be the same.[161]

---

[161] It should be pointed out that companies often issue bonds in a different currency from their own working currency. For example, iShares £ Corporate Bond (SLXX) tracks the iBoxx Sterling Liquid Long-dated Corporate Bond Index, which is currently comprised of 21 UK company issues and 34 non-UK ones. Although there is no currency exposure for investors whose domestic currency is sterling, there could be exposure to a particular country that was well represented in the index and experienced an economic crisis. This is default risk rather than currency risk.

3. Liquidity

There are a number of reasons why low liquidity poses problems with ETFs:

- An illiquid ETF may not track its index successfully and can thus move away from the net asset value (NAV) of the underlying constituents. This undermines the credentials of the ETF as an index-tracking investment.

- The prices of thinly traded ETFs are likely to be more volatile than the prices of ETFs with higher trading volumes. This makes the timing of ETF purchases and sales more significant.

- Better liquidity tends to reduce risk of trading or market-making in the ETF's shares and this will normally have the effect of reducing the bid/offer spread of the ETF. This is more of a problem for frequent traders than longer-term investors, but high spreads can more than cancel out the advantages of low expense ratios.

Discussion about the liquidity of exchange traded funds is complicated because for ETFs liquidity works on two separate levels (illustrated in Figure 8.4):

1. The first level is that of the trading volume in the secondary market for the ETF. This liquidity can have an affect on how closely the ETF tracks the NAV of its index, but particularly affects the volatility of its prices and the bid/offer spread.

2. The second type of liquidity is the liquidity of the ETF's constituents. Liquidity on this level has a greater effect on an ETF's tracking than on price volatility or spreads.

Figure 8.4 – Locating liquidity problems in an ETF

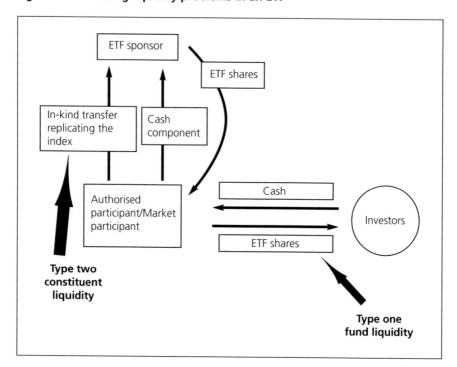

Type one liquidity: in the ETF shares

The liquidity of an ETF's shares is naturally important to market-makers and this may have implications for investors. For example, on some European exchanges it is permissible to have just one market-maker for an ETF, but bid/offer spreads tend to be wider where there is only one market-maker. If the ETF's trading volumes are great enough to attract more market-makers, spreads should come down.[162]

However, generally speaking, type two liquidity – the underlying liquidity of the ETF's constituents – has been considered critical for longer-term investors.

---

[162] This was the view expressed by Pietro Poletto, head of the ETF section of the London Stock Exchange Group, in an interview with IndexUniverse in December 2008. Exchanges will normally enforce an upper limit on the spread a market-maker can use.

Type two liquidity: in the ETF's constituents

The liquidity of the constituents is critical because arbitrage will not work if the creation baskets are too difficult to assemble (and redemption basket shares can't be sold easily). If arbitrage becomes too difficult, discounts or premiums to NAV will tend to rise, which will mean that the ETF shares are not tracking the index effectively. Generally it is agreed that (longer-term) investors should look at the liquidity of the underlying index rather than the ETF's own trading volume or the assets under management when assessing if liquidity might pose problems.[163]

* * *

In practical terms, ETFs do not abolish the liquidity problems of the markets they track. An ETF tracking an emerging market where trading volumes are low could still present problems for the authorised participants with the result that variation from net asset value may be substantial and the ETF price may be very volatile.[164]

In the case of swap-based ETFs the problem is slightly different. Illiquidity in trading of the constituent stocks of the index being tracked leads to problems in pricing them and hence pricing the ETF's shares becomes a difficult matter for the ETF's market-makers. In fact, bid/offer spreads for swap-based equity ETFs seem to cope better with liquidity and volatility problems in their underlying indices than ETFs based on full in-kind replication.

The plunging stock markets in the second half of 2008 provided an opportunity to assess how the liquidity of ETFs holds up in difficult circumstances. Although some of the most popular ETFs' bid/offer spreads continued to be very low, in general there was marked upward pressure on

---

[163] Logically, it would seem that an ETF should only be as liquid as the least liquid constituent of the index it tracks. In reality, the sponsor of an ETF tracking an index of mainly liquid stocks may well allow for cash to be added to the creation basket in place of a single illiquid stock – making it an *almost* full, in-kind replication.

[164] ETFs will often stipulate liquidity requirements for their constituents. For example, Market Vector's Africa ETF is a US-domiciled fund that tracks the Dow Jones Africa Titans 50 Index. One of the qualifications for inclusion in the index is for shares to have three months of average daily turnover exceeding US $1m.

spreads. In the US the proportion of ETFs with an XLM (see box below) of greater than 5 rose from 5% to 39% in the 12 months to October 2008.[165] In some cases this will have been a result of problems in pricing the constituent stocks in the index being tracked but more often it reflected market-makers' uncertainty about their own market.[166]

Xetra Liquidity Measure (XLM)

First employed by Deutsche Boerse on Xetra, its electronic trading platform, the Xetra Liquidity Measure is becoming accepted as a way of comparing ETFs according to their spreads.

The XLM looks at the cost of a (round-trip) purchase and immediate re-sale of a notional €25,000-worth of the ETF. XLM is expressed as a number, with 1 equating to a spread percentage of 0.01%.

Some commentators suggest, as a rule of thumb, that any XLM greater than 50 (0.5%) is always too much.

Although XLM is best for comparing spreads, some commentators discuss spreads in amount per share terms, as in 'a spread of a nickel a share'.

XLM is only a gauge for bid/offer spreads and investors should *not* assume that big spreads always coincide with poor index tracking. If an ETF makes a good job of tracking an illiquid market, the investor may consider that a higher trading spread is worth it.

---

[165] Ian Salisbury, 'Market Ills, New Rules Pinch ETF Traders', *Wall Street Journal*, 6 October 2008.

[166] The following section looks at the effects of poor liquidity on fixed-income ETFs in the same period (see the example box 'When tracking breaks down' on page 77.

One advantage that ETFs have in periods of market turmoil is that they can be traded at any time during a trading day. By contrast, the sell instructions of holders of investment funds will always be executed at the same time of the afternoon. However, it may be the case that an ETF's spread changes according to the time of day. For instance, a market-maker in an ETF may be cautious about pricing early in the trading day when only a relatively small volume of the index constituents have been traded.

To sum up, when ETFs are being considered as longer-term tracking investments, liquidity first requires consideration when it comes to timing the purchase or sale of an ETF. Secondly, liquidity, or the lack of it, can affect the ETF's ability to track its index (**tracking difference**). The holder of an ETF may be more interested in the ETF's price but it is wise to keep a watch on tracking difference. Big tracking differences merit investigation as they suggest that an ETF may not be performing in the way that it is supposed to. The crux of the risk of disappearing liquidity is that although it is much talked of, it is not only unpredictable but has a tendency to occur when least expected.

The asset classes where liquidity considerations merit particular attention are emerging (and frontier) market equity ETFs, corporate bond ETFs, property ETFs and, especially, credit ETFs. By contrast, money market ETFs and most exchange traded commodities should be free of these kinds of problems.

Where to get information about liquidity

As far as the ETF itself is concerned, some information about liquidity is readily available. Services such as Bloomberg can be checked, where trading volume history can be seen in conjunction with historical price charts.[167] It is a good idea to have a yardstick of what is an acceptable trading volume. For example, how does the ETF's trading volume compare with that of Marks & Spencer shares (to take a middling FTSE 100 company with a normal trading volume of 9m to 15m shares a day)? Also, it is probably worthwhile calculating how much share capitalisation is being traded each day rather than just the number of shares traded.

---

[167] In addition, some sponsors make available latest data about the number of separate trades. iShares is especially helpful in this regard; db x-trackers has not yet begun to populate the fields for trading volume and number of trades on its fund 'overview' page. Information about trading volumes will not include trading that is off exchange.

Liquidity of ETFs that are cross-listed

Other factors complicate assessing the liquidity of an ETF. In the case of ETFs that are cross-listed on several exchanges, the trading volume data and bid/offer spreads displayed by Bloomberg, for example, will be for just one of the exchanges but the assets under management will be an aggregate figure for all the listings of that ETF. For many ETFs a significant proportion of total trading will be done off exchange and in EU member states these trades will be unreported. This off exchange trading means that liquidity is often greater than it may appear.[168]

The relative advantage and disadvantage of swap-based replication

One of the strengths of swap-based index replication is that liquidity risks are far less than in the case of full in-kind replication. With in-kind replication, liquidity problems relating to the shares of the ETF's constituents can interfere with the process of creating and redeeming shares in the ETF; the swap process circumvents this difficulty. Nevertheless, pricing a swap-based ETF can still present problems if markets are struggling to price one or more of its constituents.

On the downside, it is important to keep an eye on potential liquidity problems arising with the swap basket. In some cases the swap basket can be comprised of stocks from an entirely different region from the index being tracked. If this is the case, a sudden sharp decrease in liquidity of that market could seriously disrupt the performance of the ETF.[169]

---

[168] At the time of writing moves are afoot to introduce improvements in this area. The Committee of European Securities Regulators (CESR) has put forward a plan to create a "consolidated tape" reporting ETF trading across all platforms, including over-the-counter trading (Chris Flood, 'EU Calls For More Reporting On ETFs', *ft.com*, 1 August 2010).

[169] An often quoted example of this is a Eurostoxx 50 swap-based ETF with a swap basket comprising Japanese equities.

Checking the liquidity of the ETF constituents

The best approach with an equity ETF is to check an up-to-date list of the ETF's holdings, take a few of the stocks that are towards the lower end in terms of percentage share of the total ETF, and then look up the trading volumes of these stocks for as far as the data goes back. In running checks like this, it is helpful to have a known period of market turmoil to refer back to; it is really the worst of times that are of interest. Finding that trading in some of an ETF's smaller constituents has been thin at times is not necessarily a show-stopper but it does indicate that market participants might have difficulties with creation and redemption baskets, that spreads on the ETF could broaden, and/or that the ETF may have problems tracking its index.

For some fixed-income ETFs there is an extra complication. With many corporate bonds, for example, thin trading levels are the norm, once the initial flurry of interest when the bond is issued has died down. While it is worth checking trading volumes for the ETF itself, uncovering low trading volumes for its constituents may not necessarily be a cause for concern. The iShares website (**www.ishares.com**) can be consulted to check how well a fixed-income ETF tracks its net asset value.

Extra market makers make a difference

Some exchanges, particularly European ones, allow stocks (and ETFs) to be traded with a single market-maker. However, the presence of a second or third market-maker will probably keep bid/offer spreads down.

ETF sponsors should provide the information about the number of market-makers for each ETF on each exchange, which could be as many as a dozen. In the case of ETFs with multiple listings, even if a particular exchange only has one market-maker, the existence of other market-makers on other exchanges should help to make spreads competitive.

Chapter 9

ETFs in the Wider Investment Context

In this chapter we will look at how ETFs compare to other investments and think about the possible future part to be played by ETFs in the UK investment scene.

Perceptions of low risk and high risk ETFs

As we have seen throughout the book, there are varying degrees of risk attached when making different ETF investments. For this reason, it makes sense to give a summary of those ETFs that can be considered generally low risk and those that can be considered generally high risk. What is under consideration here is not only risk in its pure forms (investment risk, currency risk, liquidity risk and so on) but risk that arises from the complexity of the product.

Low risk ETFs

Although every ETF carries its own investment risk, the types of ETF that are likely to be seen favourably as being at the low risk end of the range include the following:

- equity index trackers for developed markets (including fundamentally weighted and equally weighted indices as well as cap weighted ones)

- exchange traded commodities for precious metals (although at various times governments have made it difficult for investors to hold gold)[170]

- fixed-income ETFs for sovereign debt, investment grade corporate bonds and ETFs that track aggregate indices for bonds denominated in the investor's own currency

- cash or money market ETFs in the investor's own currency.

---

[170] Even if it is confirmed that the fund does represent holdings of the physical metal, a gold ETF is not quite the same asset as gold in your hand in crisis conditions, when gold is supposed to come into its own.

High risk ETFs

At the other end of the scale are the following kinds of ETF:

- all ETCs except those for precious metals – for the following reasons:

  1. Commodity indices are relatively complex in their construction and how they function.

  2. There seems to be insufficient research into whether these ETCs should or should not be combined with holdings in raw material producers' equity.

  3. The legislative and regulatory jury still seems to be out on whether investor speculation in commodities is a welcome development.

- fixed-income ETFs invested in high-yield, low-rated bonds.

- leveraged and inverse ETFs.

- frontier market equity indices.

This is not to say these higher risk ETFs should be avoided at all times, but rather that extra research should be undertaken.

Comparing ETFs with other UK collective investments

The ETF scene is changing fast all the time so it is all the more important to keep in sight the strengths that won exchange traded funds advocates and supporters early on and on which, looking ahead, the case for ETF investing will rest. These considerations are summarised in Table 9.1

Table 9.1 – ETF comparison with other UK collective investments

	ETFs	Investment funds	Investment trusts
Number of index-tracking funds	Very high	Only a small proportion of the total funds are trackers.	A very low number of tracker funds.
Choice of asset types	Very broad	Broad	Mostly equities but with a few commodities and fixed-interest funds.
All day tradability	Yes	No – just once a day.	Yes
Frequency of publication of holdings	Daily (except for some active ETFs).	Normally half-yearly.	Normally half-yearly.
Discounts or premiums to NAV	Many ETFs trade at a very low discount or premium to NAV.	Normally discounts or premiums to NAV should be minimal.	High or very high discounts or premiums to NAV are characteristic of investment trusts.
Expenses	Typically, ETF expenses will be less than 1% and sometimes much less.	Initial charges tend to be in the region of 5% unless funds are purchased through a fund supermarket.	Expense ratios vary with about half of the UK's investment trusts having expenses of less than 2.5% and one-third less than 1.5%.
Bid – offer spreads	For popular ETFs tracking well-known indices these can be very low but increase in the case of ETFs tracking more obscure asset types.	Unit trusts have significant bid-offer spreads; can be 5% or more. OEICs operate with single pricing.	Spreads should normally be less than 2%.
Fully invested	Yes	No – investment funds are required to keep a proportion of capital in cash in order to be able to repay investors when they redeem their units/shares.	Normally yes, but managers may retain some cash.
Gearing	ETFs have no mechanism for borrowing cash.	Fund managers are prevented from gearing by law.	Gearing is a tactic that many investment trust managers use.

These points of comparison will not all be viewed in the same light by all members of the investing community. Gearing, for instance, may be seen variously as injecting investment trusts with extra flexibility or as bringing unwanted risk.[171] Likewise, the all day tradability of ETFs and investment trusts has advocates and critics. It is worth noting that major shareholders in investment trusts are beginning to show willingness to force share buy backs through trusts' general meetings as one way around the problem of long-running discounts to NAV.

Overall ETFs compare very favourably with other models of collective investment on several characteristics, in particular on the points of low expenses, the choice of index tracking investments, low premiums/discounts to NAV, high transparency in relation to underlying assets and low spreads. However, there is always the danger that modifications to the original ETF designs could lead to tampering with these key strengths and could undermine the ETF case. Low expenses and good transparency appear to be especially vulnerable. Furthermore, improvements to investment funds, such as the lower charges and greater choice of index trackers being introduced to the UK by Vanguard, could have a major impact on the relative merits of these funds when considered against ETFs.

Financial advisers and ETFs

As ETFs do not carry the same commissions as investment funds, financial commentators have drawn the conclusion that financial advisers who are paid by commission are unlikely to have much time for them. Some have argued that, in the UK, financial advisers will be more keen to promote ETFs to their clients once fee-based advice has become more widespread in the wake of the Retail Distribution Review and the new requirements for giving advice on the whole market of investment products have been introduced. However, the real problem for financial advisers providing bespoke advice on ETF investing is that each ETF could require a great deal of research because of the problems of transparency and multiple areas to be researched, such as index method, liquidity and exchange rate effects.

As advisers have a fiduciary duty to their clients, recommending active funds, which have a duty to maximise returns, fits in well with periodic client

---

[171] Of course, leveraged ETFs and short leveraged ETFs, in their ability to raise risk, more than make up for the inability of ETFs to take on gearing.

portfolio reviews. Passive ETFs only have one duty: to track their index. Deciding whether or not an ETF tracker investment is in the best interest of a client appears to leave financial advisers with a lot more work to do *while the investment is held*.

If advising clients on investing in individual ETFs is broadly considered to be too onerous, it is likely that there will be considerable scope for a breed of *fund of ETFs managers* (managers who run funds whose assets are comprised of investments in ETFs). Investing through that kind of channel will increase the expense to investors but should be cheaper than investing in funds of mutual funds.

Possible future developments

This section will look at how ETF investing is likely to develop over the next decade and what effect this will have on investing in general. There are categories of investment that ETFs have yet to venture into, but the appearance of ETFs in these areas remains contingent on the development of appropriate indices. One area that could see significant growth is agricultural land or renewable forest indices and ETFs to track them.

One of the early ETF success stories was the Tracker Fund of Hong Kong and its story may contain some pointers for uses to which ETFs may be put in the future. The origins of this fund lay in the acquisition by the Hong Kong government of large numbers of shares in companies quoted on the territory's stock market in response to the Asian financial crisis in 1998. The Tracker Fund, launched with an **initial public offering** (IPO) in November 1999, was a neat solution to the problem of disposing of these assets in an orderly fashion. There may be similar operations in years to come as governments look at ways to wind down quantitative easing policies. More generally, scope for a new generation of ETFs exists in developing markets where foreign investment is wanted but foreign management is suspect.

ETFs and mutual funds

The growing popularity of ETFs at the expense of active mutual funds in particular has already been noted. The reducing of mutual fund expense ratios for active mutual funds is one likely consequence of mutual funds' attempts to increase their competitiveness and a number of other factors may combine to reduce the distinctiveness of ETFs. Some mutual fund managers such as Vanguard already offer ETFs as part of their range of investment products. The acquisition of iShares by Blackrock created another fund manager that spans the ETF-mutual fund divide. In the active area efforts will continue to develop better active ETFs and the result is likely to be a hybrid ETF/mutual fund. Regulators will subject both kinds of fund to the same tests.

Overall, professional investors and mutual funds already have a poor record for enforcing good corporate governance, so increasing popularity for ETFs is unlikely to make a great deal of difference to the general picture. However, a further substantial increase in the popularity of equity ETFs could lead to corporate governance becoming poorer still unless ETF sponsors begin to take their shareholder responsibilities more seriously.[172]

How regulation of ETFs could be improved

In the UK, with the crumbling of the occupational pension scheme system and the arrival of self-invested personal pensions, the scope for these kinds of investment seems enormous. At the same time the regulatory system, with its focus on the role of intermediaries, seems inadequate given the importance of pensions investments to the entire social fabric.

Regulation of the ETF market needs to be focused to a far greater extent on the provision of information. We have looked at the unexpected pitfalls of commodity index tracking and leveraged and short ETFs. Another aspect of ETF investing that deserves more attention is the extent to which ETF spreads and dealing costs will eat into any profit when selling ETF shares – in other words, it should be considered how frequent is too frequent when it comes to ETF trading.

The extra flexibility that ETFs can give also needs to be borne in mind and there is no to rush into making long-term decisions on how to use a given year's ISA allowance. For example, a high grade corporate bond ETF could be used as a holding strategy to avoid losing the ISA allowance. This leaves

---

[172] In the US the record of ETF sponsors in voting at shareholder general meetings is beginning to receive more attention.

plenty of time to decide what to do with the ISA long term and the switch to a long-term choice of ETF can be made when the background research is complete.

The next few decades are likely to see many more people becoming responsible for their own long-term financial well-being. It would be good if this expansion in itself was an incentive for an improvement in the investment information available, but many of the players and commentators have an interest in making ETF investing look as simple as possible and so it might not be in their interest to make more detailed information about ETFs available.

Developments in the provision of information that would be welcome include the following:

- Greater transparency about the benefits accruing to the ETF sponsor from events such as rights issues and takeovers, and how these are shared with the ETF itself.

- More specialised ETF commentary in Europe. Europe is a long way behind the US in this regard. The kind of independent assessments that would be helpful include stress testing scenarios for new funds. User-friendly summaries of sponsors' disclosures relating to risk would also be useful, especially for overseas investments.

- Rules about publishing data on ETF's tracking difference and tracking error to make it easier for comparisons between ETFs and sponsors to be made.

- Also, a joint responsibility between sponsors and newspaper publishers to correct errors of fact about an ETF when they make it into print, and for there to be tighter requirements for journalists and commentators to disclose their own holdings when writing about ETFs.

- In the UK one or more dedicated ETF online brokers (fund supermarkets).

There is one final enhancement to ETFs that would be useful, but which does not relate directly to fund information:

- All SIPP providers should be required to include **cost averaging** options for pension savers at a small additional dealing cost.

Other considerations for the future

There remain a number of largely unexplored aspects to passive investing in general and ETFs in particular. For example, if trackers continue to grow at the expense of actively managed funds, it is not clear what will happen when the first major takeover is thwarted by the sheer number of target company shares in the hands of ETFs (and other passive funds). Also, it is not known what constitutes fair treatment for ETF shareholders if a stock in the index undergoes a big reduction in its free float or qualifies for stock capping for the first time. Neither is it clear how an ETF behaves in a rights issue, as we examined in part one. A headless creature like a tracking fund is not programmed to exploit these sorts of event.[173]

In April 2010, a further ETF conundrum appeared with the news that Morgan Stanley was to start creating units in Source ETFs specifically to make more ETF shares available for stock lending to hedge funds to be used for shorting. This move away from ETF creations and redemptions being used to arbitrage differences between an ETF and its index constituents would appear to put ETFs' index tracking in doubt.

---

[173] When it comes to less weighty matters such as ETF share consolidations, it looks as if the ETF's sponsor may take a lead. For example, IndexUniverse introduced the possibility of a share consolidation for Direxion Russell 1000 Financials Bearish 3X ETF (FAZ), a leveraged inverse ETF whose precipitous fall in value meant that even very low trading spreads of two cents a share had become a significant cost in trading terms. (Matthew Hougan, 'Trading Costs and ETFs...', IndexUniverse, 5 June 2009.)

Conclusion

The advent of ETFs may have profound consequences for the finance industry and attitudes towards personal saving. *But are ETFs making investing easier?*

The answer is emphatically *yes* in that the ETF investment transaction is straightforward and many more classes of assets are opened up. Yet the affirmation needs to be qualified; while ETFs are empowering they require careful handling.

To assess the extent of this need for careful handling, it may help to turn our attention back to traditional investment funds and recognise that these investments have always involved a delegation of choices to the fund managers. Investors in investment funds have traditionally paid for the fund managers to take care of such issues as the frequency of dealing and dealing costs, liquidity problems, and exchange rate risks. By contrast, with ETFs the investor is now assuming more responsibility for these choices.

Appendix

Glossary

Glossary terms are highlighted in the text at first mention. Some terms that may be useful for readers when researching ETFs, but which are not used in the text, are included here for further reference.

5/10/40 rule

No single security may exceed 10% of a UCITS NAV, while the total number of holdings exceeding 5% of the UCITS NAV may not cumulatively exceed 40% of NAV.

accumulating ETF

An ETF tracking a non total-return index but re-investing dividends in the fund rather than paying them out to shareholders. The abbreviations AC or Acc are used in the names of accumulating ETFs.

active ETF

An ETF whose holdings are, at any stage after launch, altered as a direct result of manager intervention that cannot be predicted from the fund's objectives. (See also 'quantitative and 'quantitative-active ETFs').

arbitrage

The technique of making profits out of price differentials obtaining between different markets. In the context of ETFs this is the key driver ensuring that an ETF tracks its index efficiently, by providing the incentive to create ETF shares when the fund diverges upwards from its index and to redeem ETF shares when the fund diverges downwards from the index.

back load

A fee charged by some mutual funds when investors come to sell their holdings. Normally back load fees operate on a declining scale according to how long the investor has held their units. Investors in ETFs avoid back load (often called exit fees). Back load for ordinary investors should not be confused with the **redemption fees** charged by sponsors to participants in the ETF primary market.

base currency

The currency in which an ETF's underlying assets are denominated. This can be different from the ETF's trading currency and/or its index currency. Some

ETFs can have more than one base currency. English usage varies between sponsors and commentators in this area.

book value

A measure used by fundamental indices. Book value is calculated by adding current and fixed assets and deducting debt and liabilities and is often expressed in terms of an amount for each ordinary share (price to book ratio).

BuyWrite ETF

See 'covered call ETF'.

cash-based replication

This is a term with plenty of potential for confusion. For many commentators and industry players *cash-based* is synonymous with in-kind replication; cash is used to purchase the company shares that go into the creation basket. However, in-kind ETF creation baskets normally contain an element of cash to cover outstanding dividends. Furthermore, sponsors will sometimes accept cash in the creation basket in lieu of some or all of the shares in companies in the index. In view of this it seems to be unnecessarily confusing to refer to in-kind replication as cash-based.

closed end

American closed-end funds are similar in nature to investment trusts in the UK, both having fixed numbers of shares. Like investment trusts, closed-end fund shares often trade at a discount to their net asset value. Occasionally US commentators refer to 'closed-end exchange traded funds'; these should not be confused with ETFs.

collared weighting

A hybrid form of index weighting. Stocks in an index are tracked according to their market cap weightings unless these move too far out of alignment from the stock's fundamental weightings. Once this happens the collar comes into operation. The strategy's leading proponents are Sanjay Arya and Paul Kaplan of Morningstar.

collateral yield

Interest earned by assets used as collateral and forming a component of the return of ETCs. This is collateral posted by the investor in commodities futures contracts.

commodity ETF

An ETF that invests in the shares of raw material producing companies. Sometimes used to mean a fund that invests in commodities, in other words an exchange traded commodity.

correlation

A measure of the extent to which two investments move in step. Perfect correlation is expressed as +1; -1 signifies perfect negative correlation with the two investments always moving in opposite directions; and 0 signifies perfect non-correlation. Perfect correlation is rare but significant positive correlation is both quite common and, in the view of many portfolio management strategists, undesirable because it equates to increased risk.

cost averaging

A popular tactic for mutual fund investors is spreading the purchase of units in a fund over a number of instalments to avoid adverse effects such as paying an unnecessarily high price one day or missing out on a good (low) price while waiting until a larger number of units can be bought. Cost averaging does not really work for ETF investors because the benefits could be cancelled out by the additional commission incurred through trading more frequently.

cost basis

Also referred to as 'cost base'. This is the floor above which a taxable capital gain from a sale of shares is calculated. In the US investors in mutual funds (and ETFs) are liable for the (realised) capital gains of the fund because these gains are always distributed to investors. The in-kind creation and redemption process enables ETFs to flush out those of their holdings with the lowest cost basis and this can make them significantly more tax efficient than ordinary mutual funds.

counterparty risk

Counterparty risk (the risk of a counterparty defaulting) is that which one is exposed to when trading directly with another party rather than through a regulated exchange where trades are centrally cleared. In the context of ETFs, counterparty risks should be highlighted in the sponsor's prospectus and are most likely to arise with swap-based replication methods. However, UCITS III limits counterparty exposure to 10%, the exposure is usually collateralised and there have been recent moves to introduce multiple swap counterparties, which should also reduce counterparty risk (see **ETF Exchange**).

covered call ETF

Also called a BuyWrite ETF. Many ETFs may take advantage of returns from stock lending as a subsidiary income stream for their holders. A covered call ETF takes this one stage further in that investors are not hoping for the ETF to move up in value in the wake of its index but that the ETF will generate income from the sale of covered call options at a set price. In exchange for revenue generated from the price of the covered calls, the ETF's investors part with any improvement in the index beyond the strike level. (Example: Powershares' S&P500 BuyWrite ETF.)

creation fee

A fee charged to authorised participants for creating units in an ETF. Sponsors often stipulate a fee in the event that the creation basket is smaller than their preferred size. Creation fees can be in the order of 3% of the basket's value, so they act as an effective deterrent.

creation unit

The bulk units used in the ETF creation and redemption process. Creation unit sizes are usually stipulated by the ETF sponsor and range from 10,000 to 50,000 ETF shares in size.

creation unit holders

Synonymous with authorised participants.

cross-listing

Listing an ETF on two or more exchanges. The practice has become commonplace in Europe but which, for legal reasons, is much less common in the United States.

designated sponsor

Not an ETF sponsor in the normal sense but a market-maker in the XTF sector of the Deutsche Boerse.

discount to NAV

A ETF trading at a per share price of less than its NAV is at a discount to its NAV.

distributor status

See 'reporting status'.

efficient market hypothesis (EMH)

The influential and controversial theory that, at any time, share prices reflect all relevant information about the stock and that, therefore, it is not possible to consistently beat the market. Efficient market hypothesis (EMH) is part of the intellectual underpinning for strategies that favour tracking rather than active management. The theory was first expounded by Professor Eugene Fama in the 1960s. Somewhat counter-intuitively, EMH argues that stock markets are highly unpredictable. (See **random walk**.)

equity linked swap (ELS)

The type of swap agreement used for swap-based replication by sponsors such as Lyxor ETF and db x-trackers.

ETF Exchange

The ETF Exchange was launched by ETF Securities (ETFS) as a platform for swap-based replication of indices with multiple counterparties. The ETF Exchange was established in early 2009 with 15 European banks participating. (See 'counterparty risk'.)

exchange traded note (ETN)

ETNs are listed debt securities whose value is linked to the performance of an index but where, unlike an ETF, there is no underlying asset. ETNs carry high credit risk as the investor is fully exposed to the risk of default by the note issuer. In the past there has been some confusion between ETNs (which often track commodity indices) and exchange traded commodities properly so called. A European-domiciled ETC will normally track its index by means of a swap agreement. Although it carries counterparty risk, this should be mainly collateralised.

extraMARK

The former ETF segment of the London Stock Exchange.

free float adjustment

The adjustment of a cap-weighted stock index to reflect the proportion of shares in a company that can realistically be expected to be for sale. Normally long-standing government stakes or shares issued as part of an employee share option scheme would not be considered as part of the free float.

front load

Front end fees charged to investors in mutual funds. Investors purchasing ETF shares on the secondary market are not subject to this type of charge.

front running

A term with a number of different but related meanings. The broadest meaning is share trading on the basis of information that has not yet entered into the public domain. This includes the illegal practice of a broker trading in a stock on their own behalf before effecting a client's order, in the expectation that the client's trade will move the share price. In the context of ETFs, front running refers to the threat that full portfolio disclosure on the part of active ETFs will be imitated by other investors. As active ETFs are a very new phenomenon, this kind of front running is more of a perception than a reality.

gearing

The American term for leverage.

grantor trust

A US type of exchange traded fund. Grantor trusts are distinct from normal ETFs because they have static constituents, so there is no rebalancing to track an index but no expense ratios either. Investors are treated as the beneficial owners of, and enjoy voting rights for, the underlying stocks. Any investor can redeem the underlying stocks – not just authorised participants. The best known grantor trusts are HOLDRS. From a regulatory point of view grantor trusts are treated as a form of **unit investment trust (UIT)**.

hair cut

In the context of swap-based ETFs, an adjustment to the valuation of the collateral provided by the swap counterparty, normally requiring a like adjustment to the amount of the collateral provided.

HOLDRS

A trust–issued receipt that represents beneficial ownership of a specified group of stocks. HOLDRS allow investors to benefit from the ownership of stocks in a particular industry, sector or group. See **grantor trust**.

index currency

The currency used by an index compiler/publisher to measure the index. For a national index the index currency will normally be the currency of the country in question. For international indices the index currency is normally the dollar, or in the case of European indices, such as the DJ STOXX 600, the euro.

Index Strategy Boxes
An ETF analysis tool developed by Nick Ferri of Portfolio Solutions. The Index Strategy Boxes are essentially a grid with three types of security selection on the x axis – quantitative, screened and passive – and three different weighting systems on the y axis – market cap, fundamental and fixed weight. The tool is frequently used in order to compare ETF expense ratios as well as the success of different investment strategies.

indicative optimized portfolio value
IOPV is the US counterpart to iNAV or intraday indicative value.

initial public offering
ETFs can raise funds by way if an IPO, although in Europe the seeding of the ETF is normally provided entirely by the sponsor and the fund begins life on the exchange with a simple listing. There are also IPO ETFs such as the First Trust IPOX-100 Index ETF (FPX) that tracks US IPOs from their seventh to their 1000th day.

in-kind replication
The kind of replication used in the creation and redemption processes in which the ETF's assets are the same as the assets whose performance the ETF tracks.

Intellidex
An index brand of the American Stock Exchange that is licensed to Invesco Powershares and tracked by a number of their ETFs.

intraday indicative value
IIV is an indicator of the net asset value of the assets being tracked by the ETF, provided at intervals throughout the day.

inverse ETF
An ETF that tracks the inverse of the daily price performance of an index.

issuing company
Synonymous with **sponsor**.

leveraged ETF

An ETF that uses financial derivatives and debt to multiply the returns of an underlying index in its returns.

life-cycle ETF

An ETF that tracks a life cycle indice (also known as a target date indice). These are indices that follow investment strategies deemed to be appropriate for the life stages of the investor. Typically, these involve (relatively) aggressive investing for younger investors (when there is plenty of time to make up for investment setbacks) and progressively more cautious strategies as the subject approaches retirement. Therefore these indices (and the ETFs that track them) tend to switch progressively from equities into fixed-income securities. Although this approach has wide currency among advisers, there have been warnings that it could prevent older investors from achieving substantial gains if, say, their last decade before retirement is a period of stock market gains.

limit orders

An order for a stock purchase or stock sale where, respectively, the maximum price or minimum price is stipulated by the client.

market-timing (scandal)

Market-timing is the practice of taking advantage of out-of-date net asset value data for – in particular – mutual funds investing in overseas markets. Units in mutual funds investing in, say, Far Eastern equities, will be priced on the basis of the closing prices that are hours old. On days where a stock market rise is expected in the Far East on the following day (say in response to a strong performance in the Dow or the S&P 500) those in the know may buy units one day and sell them the next at a profit. If the staff of mutual funds that, publicly, are committed to not engaging in such practices do engage in them, it constitutes a fraud. Although ETFs tracking overseas markets have the same problem providing net asset values, the fact that they are trading continuously makes their share prices much more responsive to next day forecasts for the overseas market. This makes market-timing impossible.

master unit

Alternative name for ETFs used by Lyxor Asset Management. However, their 2009 brochure does not use the term.

Most, Nathan (1914-2004)

The designer of the first SPDR in 1991. He took the idea to Vanguard who declined to take an interest but State Street Bank saw the potential.

net asset value (NAV)

The assets of an investment fund or investment trust minus its liabilities, normally expressed on a per share or per unit basis. NAV is normally expressed in the fund's index currency. ETFs are supposed to trade at a price close to the NAV of the underlying index they track. See also 'discount to NAV' and 'premium to NAV'.

noisy market hypothesis

Another contribution to the debate about how accurately equity markets capture information relating to share prices, developed by Jeremy Siegel in an article in the *Wall Street Journal* in 2006. The basic idea is that traders and investors impute value to particular stocks for various faulty reasons and that cap-weighted indices reflect this noise. Siegel's conclusion was that fundamentally weighted indices and dividend weighting in particular would guide investors away from market noise in the future.

open-ended fund/investment

A collective investment in which the number of shares or units is not fixed. Shares or units are created in response to investor demand and cancelled when investors redeem their investments. The consequences of this are, firstly, that discounts and premiums to NAV are avoided; secondly, the fund has to liquidate holdings when investors wish to redeem their shares in the fund; and, thirdly, the fund's growth or shrinkage is affected by investor demand for the shares as well as changes in the value of its holdings.

optimisation/optimised replication

See 'representative sampling strategy'

(ETF) options

Trading in ETF options is a growing form of derivatives trading on the Euronext-NYSE-Liffe and Eurex markets.

partial in-kind replication

See 'representative sampling strategy'.

performance difference

see 'tracking difference'.

permanent liquidity providers

Another name for market-makers.

physical replication

This can be synonymous with in-kind replication but, given that an in-kind creation basket will probably consist of dematerialised (.ie. non-paper) share certificates, this seems to be stretching the meaning of the word 'physical' too far. Physical replication may also refer to the assets of some precious metal ETCs, that is bullion in a vault, and this seems a perfectly proper description of that kind of ETC.

portfolio deposit

Loosely meaning the same as creation unit, but more accurately refers to the equity component in an in-kind replication as opposed to any cash component.

premium to NAV

An ETF trading at a per share price of greater than its NAV is at a premium to its NAV.

price index

An index that does not show total returns.

price-weighted index

An index like the Dow Jones Industrial Average where the index is an average of the share prices of the constituents.

pure style indices

A range of ETFs from Rydex of the US that track indices of stocks selected for growth or value style characteristics where the weighting is according to style scores rather than market cap.

quantitative and quantitative-active ETFs

Quantitative analysis uses measurables from corporate accounts for assessing equities. It is a particularly important tool for designing fundamentally weighted or equally weighted indices and analysing their performance with a view to creating quantitative ETFs to track them. Quantitative-active ETFs may only be active in the sense of changing their constituent holdings more frequently than passive funds, but may also allow the ETF manager more discretion in making the final stock selections, albeit from shortlists produced by computer models.

random walk

A Random Walk Down Wall Street is the title of a hugely influential book by Burton Malkiel, first published in 1973. Malkiel's argument is that asset prices typically demonstrate randomness in their movement and that active investment strategies in general, and strategies based on fundamentals in particular, do not outperform passive strategies over time.

redemption fees

Sometimes charged by the sponsor to authorised participants, these are the equivalent of creation fees but at the redemption stage.

(interference) reflexivity

The theory proposed by George Soros, the renowned financier, that objective statements cannot be made about investment because the statements will (probably) have an effect on what they purport to merely describe. Soros's argument is that because of reflexivity, markets are inefficient, do not naturally return to equilibrium and are dependent on effective regulation. Implicit in Soros's approach is the belief that there are identifiable trends with consequences that can be partly forecasted – if you can spot and make due allowance for the interference reflexivity at work – and that, therefore, active investment strategies can be successful.

replication basis

The relationship between the ETF NAV (on a per share basis) and the index value, normally expressed as a fraction. So, if an ETF has a replication basis of 1/100 and the index tracked stands at 4450, the ETF's NAV should be 44.50 a share.

reporting status

Designation of investment funds including ETFs and ETCs that affects whether capital gains are subject to capital gains tax or income tax. Without reporting status (or distributor status as it was formerly known) an ETF shareholder will be liable for income tax on the ETF's capital gains. Fund fact sheets should indicate whether or not an ETF has reporting status; most LSE-listed ETFs do have it.

representative sampling strategy

A variation on full in-kind replication. Optimised replication seeks to capture the performance of an index by partial in-kind replication of the constituents. Rather than buying the whole index, an ETF's managers will buy a sample of the index constituents that will perform in broadly the same way as the whole index. This can reduce costs where the number of index constituents is very high and avoid problems with buying and selling index constituents that are illiquid. iShares is the leading proponent of this method of ETF construction.

roll on

The key mechanism of a commodities index calculated from futures contracts. The contracts are by definition fixed term so the index has to link them in sequences. The joins in the sequence are known as roll ons, which can either be in 'contango' – the further contract is more expensive than the current one – or in 'backwardation' – the nearer contract is the more expensive.

sector rotation

Investment strategies that exploit the fact that different sectors of the equity market prosper at different times and, in particular, that these differences in performance are partly related to the stages of the economic cycle. In the US Claymore/Zacks and Powershares both sponsor ETFs that perform sector rotation strategies.

segment indices

Cap-weighted indices differentiated by size such as the Russell 1000 Large Cap and the Russell 2000 Small Cap.

short ETF

See 'inverse ETF'.

sondervermoegen

A category of collective investment instrument found in Germany and Switzerland that can cover ETF and ETC-like funds.

source ETF

Similar to ETF Exchange in being a collaborative effort, launching a range of swap-based ETFs domiciled in Europe with multiple counterparties. The difference here is that the initiative came from the swap counterparties, not the sponsor. The venture was created by Goldman Sachs and Morgan Stanley and subsequently joined by Bank of America Merrill Lynch.

SPDR ('Spiders')

S&P Depositary Receipts, the first US ETF, launched by State Street.

sponsor

The company or financial institution which creates and administers an exchange-traded fund.

stock capping

A mechanism to prevent any company or companies dominating a cap-weighted index by preventing the weighting of any company being allowed to rise above a set percentage.

stock lending

ETF sponsors using the in-kind replication, as holders of large numbers of equities, may engage in stock lending to provide an additional source of returns to fund shareholders and this is an additional source of risk for investors (which should be spelled out in the prospectus). In the case of swap-based ETFs, the swap counterparty may use the substitute basket for stock-lending purposes but the ETF shareholder has no direct exposure to the risks involved.

style drift

A departure from the investment strategy proposed by a mutual fund at its inception. Most ETFs avoid this kind of evolution, which all actively managed funds are vulnerable to.

substitute basket

The basket of assets delivered by the sponsor of a swap-based ETF to the swap counterparty in return for which the swap counterparty guarantees tracking of the relevant index for the ETF shares created.

synthetic replication

As opposed to in-kind replication; most often using swaps but possibly based on other types of derivative such as futures contracts.

teeter-totter

A product structure developed by MacroShares whereby a pair of exchange traded tracking products is created: a long version and a short version for the same index. The underlying assets are shifted between the two funds depending upon whether the tracked index rises or falls. To date such products have been leveraged ones and have fixed expiry dates unless (as a result of leveraging) one of the pair hits zero.

total expense ratio (TER)

The sponsor's management fee. TER differences between various ETFs, and between ETFs and other types of investment such as mutual funds, are an important selling point. They are calculated and accrue to the sponsor on a daily basis, so there is no way for an ETF investor to avoid them.

total return index

An equity index where the dividends and other distributions are incorporated or a commodities index where the interest on an element of the value of the futures contracts that would not be required for margin (and could therefore be invested in government paper) is incorporated. In the case of most equity indices the dividends are deemed to have been re-invested in the company that paid them rather than being pooled to be re-invested in proportion to the cap-weighting of the constituents.

tracking difference

The difference in the performance between a fund and its benchmark index.

tracking error

Precise definition: the standard deviation of the difference of the returns of a fund and its benchmark index. Tracking error is a phrase that is also used loosely instead of 'tracking difference' but in really tracking error is 'form' on tracking difference calculated statistically over time. At present, comparisons of tracking errors for different ETFs are not easily available.

trading currency

The currency in which an ETF is traded on a stock exchange. ETFs may have different versions that have different trading currencies.

trending market

A market where an index tracks upwards or downwards in an uninterrupted manner with few zigzags. These kind of conditions produce good returns for investors in leveraged and short ETFs, provided the trend is in the right direction.

trustee

Normally a bank acting as custodian of an ETF's assets.

underlying asset

This is straightforward for ETFs where replication is of the full in-kind variety; the underlying asset is both the index tracked and the contents of the creation baskets that go into the ETF. In the case of the swap-based ETF the underlying asset is the index tracked, not the actual assets of the ETF. Somewhat confusingly, in the case of inverse ETFs, commentators will talk of the index whose performance is being inverted as the underlying asset.

unit investment trust (UIT)

The legal form of some US ETFs. The characteristics of a UIT are: a once and for all issue of units; a fixed lifespan; a secondary market in the units maintained by the sponsor; and a fixed list of constituent holdings. The list of constituents does not change to reflect changes in the constituents of an index.

VIPERs

Vanguard Index Participation Equity Receipts. The US-domiciled ETF range of Vanguard, the highly respected passive mutual fund manager.

XTF

The ETF sector of the Deutsche Boerse, Europe's leading ETF exchange.

Major ETF Sponsors

Below is a list of the principal European and North American ETF sponsors. Although some sponsors have ETFs with multiple stock exchange listings, which are tradable in more than one currency, reference to more than one exchange or more than one currency in this list is not intended to indicate that all of a provider's funds are available on each exchange or in each currency.

Sponsor	Comment	First launch	Number of funds	Exchanges	Replication method	UCITS' compliant
Amundi (formerly CASAM)	CASAM was an acronym for Credit Agricole Structured Asset Management, which also markets structured products and alternative investments in addition to ETFs. CASAM focuses almost entirely on equity ETFs (including sector, style and inverse) although it also sponsors a money market ETF and four ETCs.	2001	88	NextTrack Euronext Paris Borsa Italiana Deutsche Boerse	Swap-based	Yes
BMO financial		2009	4	Toronto	Swap-based	No
Charles Schwab	A well-known US broker and mutual fund supermarket that moved into ETFs in 2009. The offer to clients of its other services of ETF trading free of dealing charges attracted significant attention.	2009	8	NYSE Arca	In-kind replication or representative in-kind replication	No
Claymore Securities*	All but six of Claymore's ETFs are equity funds, the exceptions being an aggregate bond fund and a short-term bond. The ETFs focus on a number of different strategies such as dividend optimisation and sector rotation. Most Claymore ETFs are sponsored in partnership with index compilers. Claymore announced its merger with Guggenheim Partners at the end of July 2009.	2006	52	NYSE Arca, Toronto	Substantial in-kind, or representation	No

Comstage	Part of Commerzbank of Germany. Most of Comstage's ETFs, which are domiciled in Luxembourg, are equity ETFs, but they also sponsor some fixed-income and cash ETFs.	2008	80	Xetra[174] DeutscheBoerse (Frankfurt & Stuttgart)	Swap-based	Yes
Credit Suisse	A range of ETFs formerly sold under the XMTCH brand, but now known simply as Credit Suisse ETFs, covering mainly the Swiss equity and government bond markets. For information, search for Credit Suisse ETFs rather than the main Credit Suisse website.	2001	86	SIX Swiss Exchange (and two funds are traded on the Deutsche Boerse). New funds will be listed on both these exchanges together with NYSE Euronext and the Borsa Italiana. Most recently Credit Suisse has launched 45 funds on the LSE.	Originally in-kind replication (although it seems that the sponsor will accept cash subscriptions which are then used for the purchase of shares to go into the creation basket). In 2010 Credit Suisse began launching some swap-based ETFs.	
db x-trackers	Part of Deutsche Bank and Europe's leading sponsor of ETFs covering equities, bonds, credit, currency, money market and commodity indices. The ETFs are all domiciled in Luxembourg. Deutsche Bank announced the launch of a range of db ETCs in 2010. db x-trackers is also an important sponsor of Singapore and Hong Kong domiciled ETFs.	2007	100+	Xetra Deutsche Boerse, Euronext Paris, Borsa Italiana and the London Stock Exchange and the SWX Swiss Exchange	Swap-based	Yes
Direxion*	A leader in the field of leveraged and short ETFs in the US. The sponsor of the US's two most popular new ETFs in the year to June 2009, the Direxion Financial Bear X3 and the Direxion Financial Bull X3, both of which have scored substantial losses in value in the first half of 2009.	2001	40	NYSE Arca, NYSE Euronext Amsterdam	In-kind and/or cash for bull funds, cash only for bear funds.	No

---

[174] Strictly speaking these Deutsche Boerse listings are on the XTF segment, which is a subset of Xetra, but most sponsors' documentation refers to 'Xetra'.

EasyETF	A joint venture between Axa Insurance and BNP Paribas but now managed by BNP Paribas Asset Management. The ETF includes equity ETFs for sectors and emerging markets, fixed-income ETFs and credit ETFs.	2005	Circa 60	Borsa Italiana, Deutsche Boerse, Euronext Paris, Swiss Exchange	Swap-based and in-kind replication	Yes
ETFlab	ETFlab sponsors a range of equity and fixed-income ETFs, including a price only version of the DAX. The company is a subsidiary of DekaBank of Germany.	2008	30	Xetra, Deutsche Boerse	Full in-kind replication	Yes
ETF Securities	Often abbreviated to ETFS, this is the leading sponsor of commodity ETFs and ETCs and can claim credit for the invention of the latter category. ETFS is also the driving force behind ETF Exchange, a facility for providing multiple swap counterparties for an ETF.	2004	180+	Borsa Italiana, Xetra Deutsche Boerse, Euronext Amsterdam & Paris, Irish Stock Exchange & London Stock Exchange. ETFS is in the process of launching exchange traded products in the US market.	Swap-based	Yes
Global X	US ETF sponsor specialising in emerging market ETFs	2008	30	NYSE Arca	Full in-kind/representative sampling	No
Grail Advisors*	Significant as a trail blazer for truly active equity ETFs that are managed in a similar fashion to mutual funds.	2009	7	NYSE Arca	Full in-kind	No
HSBC	The most important new player in the UK ETF market.	2009	9	LSE, Euronext Paris	In-kind	Yes
Invesco Powershares (including Powershares Global Funds Ireland)	One of the largest North American sponsors and the creator of America's second most famous ETF, the QQQ, which tracks the NASDAQ-100. Powershares is the ETF arm of the company best known in the UK for its fund management business, Invesco Perpetual.	2000	113	LSE, NASDAQ and NYSE Arca	In-kind	No, except for funds listed on LSE

iShares	Probably the best known ETF brand. Formerly part of Barclays Global Investors but sold to Blackrock in 2009. iShares has distinct North American and European operations and is the largest ETF issuer in the US and worldwide. It has operations in 16 countries. It acquired Index Exchange from HypoVereinsbank in 2006.	1999	Circa 140 in Europe	Xetra Deutsche Boerse, London Stock Exchange, NYSE Arca	Mainly in-kind but German-domiciled funds are swap-based.	European domiciled funds are UCITS' compliant.
Lyxor	Part of Société Générale, Europe's second largest ETF sponsor by assets under management. Lyxor sponsors a broad range of ETFs and a few ETCs. Particular areas of strength are country and sector ETFs. Of particular note is the Lyxor ETF Wise Quantitative Strategy, which tracks a Société Générale index based on value and momentum factors.	2001	80+	Most major European stock exchanges and Hong Kong	Swap-based	Yes
MacroShares*	A leading exponent of paired long/short exchange-traded securities with fixed lifetimes.	2006	None currently	NYSE Arca	Not applicable – the assets of the paired securities are invested in US government bonds.	No
Market Vectors*	The ETF brand of Van Eck Associated of the US. Their range includes commodity ETFs, ETFs for a few emerging markets and ETFs tracking municipal bond indices.	2006	20	NYSE Arca	In-kind	No
Pimco*	The most highly respected bond mutual fund manager in the US has crossed over to fixed-income ETFs.	2009	10	NYSE Arca	In-kind	No
Proshares*	Specialises in inverse and leveraged funds.	2006	111	NYSE Arca	Multiple: in-kind sampling, swap-based, derivative-based	No

Royal Bank of Scotland, The (RBS)	Launched London's Stock Exchange listed ETFs in July 2010 with a small range of equities and commodities futures ETFs, having marketed ETFs in continental Europe under the MarketAccess brand.	2001	6 LSE listed	LSE, EuroNext, Deutsche Boerse Wiener Boerse, SIX Market, Borsa Italiana	Swap-based	Yes
Rydex*	Rydex specialises in ETFs tracking equally-weighted and style indices, and leveraged and inverse ETFs. They also own the CurrencyShares brand of funds. Rydex's parent company was acquired by Guggenheim Partners early in 2010.	2003	19	NYSE Arca	Principally in-kind replication	No
SGAM	A range of active ETFs sponsored by Société Générale Asset Management. These are ETFs that provide leveraged and inverse performance, or partial tracking with an element of capital protection. This business was absorbed by Lyxor in late 2009.	2007-9	Formerly 13 of which 8 have been merged with very similar Lyxor ETFs.	NextTrackEur-onext Paris, Borsa Italiana, Xetra Deutsche Boerse	Normally synthetic	Yes
Source ETF	A European joint venture by Bank of America, Goldman Sachs, Morgan Stanley, Banca IMI, IMC Group and Nomura to act as counterparties for swap-based ETFs. The range is based on equities and ETCs with just one money market fund. Source ETF's decision to list each ETF and ETC exclusively on one market (mainly the Xetra market but some are listed on the LSE) has been seen by some commentators as the beginning of a trend away from cross-listings for European-domiciled ETFs. Source ETF has been licensed to use the Dow Jones Euro STOXX range of indices.	2009	48	Xetra Deutsche Boerse & London Stock Exchange	Swap-based in the main but the Source DAX ETF is based on full in-kind replication	Yes but only ETFs, not ETCs
SPA Marketgrader	A range of six quantitative-active ETFs that were delisted in May 2009. SPA has said that it may re-introduce the Marketgrader approach in the future.	2007	0	LSE	In-kind	Yes

SPDR (Spiders)	The sponsor of the oldest ETF still in existence, the SPDR S&P 500 (SPY), which has assets upwards of $65bn. The SPDR range is sponsored by State Street Global Advisors (SSgA) and holds second place in the global ETF market measured by assets under management. However, in Europe State Street only holds ninth place. The information provided here is for the European-domiciled ETFs only, also known as streetTRACKS. These cover regional equity markets and sectors.	2001	13	Euronext Amsterdam (main listing) and Paris, Xetra Deutsche Boerse	In-kind	Yes
UBS	The tenth largest European ETF sponsor by assets under management. UBS branched out into ETCs in 2008.	2001	9 (plus ETCs)	Euronext Paris, Xetra Deutsche Boerse, SIX Swiss Exchange, (for ETCs only) London Stock Exchange	In-kind or swap-based or a combination of the two	No
United States Commodity Funds*	The sponsor of six energy ETCs including the much reported United States Oil Fund, United States 12 Month Oil Fund and United States Natural Gas Fund. Formerly known as Victoria Bay Asset Managament. United States Commodity Funds is part of the mutual fund manager Ameristock.	2006	8	NYSE Arca	In-kind	No
Vanguard*	The ETFs of the US's leading manager of passive mutual funds. They were sold under the VIPERS brand until 2006.	2001	46	NYSE Arca	In-kind	No
Xact Fonder	A Swedish sponsor of equity ETFs, including two that track fundamental indices.	2001	7	Stockholm Stock Exchange, Oslo Stock Exchange	In-kind or futures (for leveraged or inverse funds)	No

Sponsors marked with an * do not market their ETFs to European Union investors.

Smaller ETF Providers

ALPS (US): Known primarily for marketing and distributing ETFs to financial advisors, ALPS sponsors six ETFs of its own, five of them commodity ETFs.

BBVA (Spain and Mexico): sponsors seven ETFs in Spain.

Clal Finance (Israel): sponsors 35 ETFs under the Mabat brand.

Deutsche Boerse Commodities (Germany): The sponsor of Xetra Gold fund is a joint venture between Deutsche Boerse, a number of banks and a gold refiner.

Dexia (Luxembourg): tracks sustainability indices.

DNB NOR (Norway): sponsor of three funds for Norwegian equities.

Finans Portfoy (Turkey): sponsors six ETFs.

HQ Bank (Sweden): sponsors three ETFs.

Julius Baer (Switzerland): one gold ETF.

Marshall Wace (UK): One ETF planned copying this firm's hedge strategies.

Medvesek Pusnik (Slovenia): one ETF tracking a Europe-wide index.

Nextra (Italy): sponsor of two ETFs under the beta1 brand.

Northern Trust (USA): launched and then shut down 17 ETFs in 2007-9; now they are planning to enter ETF field again.

Osmosis Fund (UK): one climate ETF launched in 2010.

RevenueShares (US): sponsor of six revenue (sales) weighted equity ETFs.

Seligson Hex25 (Finland): one fund tracking Finnish equities.

ZKB (Switzerland): a gold ETF (with assets of 4.4bn SwFr) and a platinum ETF.

Index

ETFs are followed by their current ticker if they are still trading. Where an ETF has changed its name and/or its sponsor, the name is given as it will be found in the text. All ETFs or ETCs are London listed unless otherwise stated.